CAREERS IN
THEORY
AND
EXPERIENCE

CAREERS IN THEORY AND EXPERIENCE

A Twenty-Year Longitudinal Study

Warren D. Gribbons   **Paul R. Lohnes**

STATE UNIVERSITY OF NEW YORK PRESS
ALBANY

Published by
State University of New York Press, Albany

© 1982 State University of New York

Printed in the United States of America

For information, address State University of New York Press, State University Plaza, Albany, N.Y., 12246

Library of Congress Cataloging in Publication Data
Gribbons, Warren D.
    Careers in theory and experience.

    Bibliography: p.
    Includes index.
    1. United States—Occupations—Longitudinal
studies.   2. Vocational guidance—United States—
Longitudinal studies.   I. Lohnes, Paul R.
II. Title.
HF5382.5.U5G697   381.11'4'0973   82-762
ISBN 0-87395-611-7   AACR2
ISBN 0-87395-612-5 (pbk.)

Contents

Tables

Preface

This book completes the report on a longitudinal study of career development that has occupied the authors for more than two decades. How the pursuit of happiness, productivity, and security has occupied the 111 subjects of our study for the 21 years since we first met them in their junior high schools is the substance of our report, and without their generosity we would have had nothing to narrate.

To our subjects, then, we express our gratitude and congratulations. As a group you have been remarkably successful in your lives and careers, and by sharing your experiences with us and our readers you have enriched the knowledge base from which educators provide guidance to the nation's youth. Many of you have become our friends as well as our informants. You have shared with us the intimate details of your achievements and your losses. We have shared your thrills, your pleasure, and your pain. The impersonality of the abstract analyses of your experiences contained herein masks your individual personalities, but we trust you sense our appreciation of you as individuals. To you, our special thanks.

As our subjects know, Jean Gribbons has been a complete partner with her husband Warren in the collection of the data. Although she has left the analysis and writing to Warren and Paul, her interest in the work has made her a positive influence on all our deliberations.

Professors Donald E. Super and David V. Tiedeman provided us with invaluable leadership and encouragement. The U.S. Office of Education funded the first decade of the study. Our institutions, Regis College and the State University of New York at Buffalo, have been very supportive over the years. Many of our students (particularly Mary Clancy Allen) and friends have helped in a variety of ways. Catherine Lee and Lu Pai are acknowledged as co-authors of sections of this book. To all who have helped in this research program, our thanks.

Finally, a research report without readers is the emptiest of gestures. If you read this book you will have our gratitude. Should you wish to, we would enjoy corresponding with you.

Warren D. Gribbons   Paul R. Lohnes
Regis College   379 Baldy Hall
235 Wellesley Street   SUNY at Buffalo
Weston, MA 02193   Amherst, NY 14260

1
Exploration: A Modal Experience of Adolescence

Human behavior is the epicenter of knowledge. Humans struggle to know their natural environment better in order to know where they are and what they can do. The subjective elements of need, problem, and purpose permeate the most objective science and engineering. As mastery of our environment advances, we are increasingly aware of the importance of studying ourselves. We want to know what people do and to understand why. We need to know what to expect of people under various circumstances. Human behavior poses a greater threat to us than anything else in nature, yet at the same time, we realize that people embody nature's greatest potential.

Ultimately, we want to know what to expect of and for ourselves. It is our own behavior that is the epicenter for us. You and I can pretend that knowledge is impersonal when we converse as fellow scholars, scientists, or educators, but what does the pretense really achieve? In this study of human careers in progress we are going to try to relate to the individuality of our subjects. We will give full vent to our need to abstract, to number and count, and to analyze, but at the same time we will not deny our need to imagine, to empathize, and to moralize. We pursue scientific knowledge of career development because we want to know how to help young people in their personal struggles for career development. We are educators who want to see our schools do a better job of guiding youths toward useful and satisfying careers. We do not want this for heroic or saintly reasons but we do want it, and we are particularly interested in those among our readers who also want it.

Humans work to live. Work is a primary element of humanity's fate. It is instrumental not only in securing the necessities of life but also in conferring the status of responsible adulthood. The lucky person enjoys work and looks forward to returning to it after being away from it for a time. Our work expresses our lives in the same way that our families and our avocations do. Good work is very important to us. But, good work is not everyone's lot in this world. A person must choose and seek in order to secure good work, and he also needs some grace and some luck. If he is ill-endowed, or he judges poorly, or he blunders repeatedly, he may flounder for years or for a lifetime in a succession of wretched jobs, or he may stagnate endlessly in one detestable job, or he may become unemployable. We have neighbors whom we call "hard-core unemployables."

What may be good work for a person today is not necessarily good work tomorrow for the same person. Many people need progression in their work lives over the years. Others need at least some variety. It is not the job circumstances of the moment that individuals value so much as it is the pattern in their work history as they have already lived it and as they anticipate the future. Their deeper contentment or frustration stems from their contemplation of the long run of their affairs— what their track record has been and where they seem headed and how well they are moving. We consume our tomorrows today in the forward rush of our minds, even as we bask in, or cower from, the reflections of our yesterdays. Since a career looms larger than any single job in our lives, the career is the focus of our study of vocational development.

If it is desirable for adults to help youths in anything, it is clearly desirable that our schools offer guidance in career development. Guidance is *not* deciding for young people, but rather providing information that is essential for their own decision making. In order that we may teach valid and useful understanding of career processes we must have a basic research literature covering career development. Some years ago when Donald Super and his colleagues published *Vocational Development: A Framework for Research* (1957), there was little scientific knowledge about career development, but the buildup was already promised: The Career Pattern Study (CPS) (Super and Overstreet, 1960) had been collecting data for five years, the Career Development Study (CDS) (Gribbons and Lohnes, 1968) was starting, and Project TALENT (Cooley and Lohnes, 1968) was being planned. Today these three projects have reported a wealth of empirical information about careers, as has much other recent research. Equally important are the contributions toward a theory of career development that the investigators in CPS, CDS, TALENT, and other projects have produced. We now have a basic research literature, and it is time we addressed ourselves more widely to the implementation of career guidance practices based on this body of knowledge. Again, there are leaders already well advanced in this undertaking.

Our purpose here is to add to the basic research literature a report on the second and final stage of CDS. We have previously reported on the first half of this 20-year study, in *Emerging Careers* (Gribbons and Lohnes 1968). We need not undertake a thorough review of the literature because others have already done so (Crites 1968; Osipow 1968; Holland and Whitney 1969; Super and Hall 1978). We will review the adolescence of the CDS subjects, using freely the ideas we have assimilated from the literature. Then we will review a later report from CPS (Super, Kowalski, and Gotkin 1967), since it concerns the same period of development as this report and since CPS has always been the model for CDS. We will report our analyses of data collected four years and six years beyond high school from 110 CDS subjects and what we see as the theoretical implications of the analytical outcomes. We will then relate the experiences of CDS youths to the challenge to educators inherent in career psychology. The latest followups and the latest improvements in our instrument for measuring vocational maturity are the topics of the final chapters.

That there is a crying need for an easily administered and scored measure of vocational maturity has been amply demonstrated by the number of requests for copies of Readiness for Career Planning (RCP) that have been directed to us in past years. Recognition of this is also shown by the number of instruments developed or revised over the last decade and reported in the literature. Three of these are described very briefly below. For complete, detailed descriptions of these instruments, the reader is urged to consult Super (1974) and Jordaan and Heyde (1979).

1. Career Development Inventory (CDI) (Forest and Thompson 1974). This is an objective 91-item, paper-and-pencil inventory consisting of three scales: the planning orientation scale, the resources for exploration scale, and the information and decision making scale. Two attitude scales, a cognitive score, and a total score are obtained.

2. Career Maturity Inventory (CMI) (Crites 1974) consists of two scales: Career Choice Competencies and Career Choice Attitudes. The Career Choice Attitudes measures five attitudes central to career maturity: involvement in the choice process, orientation toward work, independence in decision making, preference for vocational choice factors, and conceptions of the choice process. It is a 50-item, pencil-and-paper inventory that can be machine- or hand-scored and yields a global score of maturity of career attitudes. The Career Choice Com-

petencies scale is made up of 100 items divided into five subtests: self-appraisal, occupational information, goal selection, planning, and problem solving.

3. The Cognitive Vocational Maturity Test (CVMT) (Westbrook and Mastie 1974) consists of 120 questions divided into six subtests: field of work, job selection, work conditions, educational requirements, attributes required, and duties. This test may be administered to a group and can be scored by teachers and counselors.

Jordaan and Heyde (1979) report on a 1972 study by Forest in which CDI, CMI, CVMT, and RCP were re-administered to a group of 10th-grade students in Michigan. He found RCP correlated .78 with the CMI Attitude Scale and .75 with the CDI Total Score. The relationship between CDI Total Score and CMI Attitude Scale was .14 and between CDI and CVMT was .26. although the sample was too small in some cases to yield definitive results, there is promising evidence that certain aspects of vocational maturity can be measured.

In a comparison between the Vocational Development Inventory (VDI) (Crites 1965), forerunner to the CMI, and RCP, Hansen and Ansell (1973) found that both instruments show an overall progression in vocational maturity and that scores from the two instruments were significantly related. Inter-rater reliability of four certified school counselors scoring RCP ranged from .87 to .98 with an average coefficient of .95, further confirming our confidence in the accuracy with which RCP can be scored.

In another report based on administration of RCP to 375 subjects, Ansell and Hansen conclude:

> The Readiness for Vocational Planning Schedule holds a promising future in vocational counseling. Rapport can be established with clients by first seeking classification information required by the instrument. Once such information is acquired, clients generally are willing to cooperate by responding to the questions requested in the interview. The total score may not necessarily be as informative as the quality of the responses offered by the clients. An item analysis of the questions relevant to the variable being assessed affords an opportunity to gain insight into the client as well as the client learning about his particular strengths and weaknesses. (1977, p. 386)

Tentative Substage of Exploration

At the beginning of the Career Development Study in early 1958, the 57 boys and 54 girls had an average age of 13.4 years and were 8th-

Table 1.1. Career Development Stages

I. **Growth Stage (birth–14)**
1. Fantasy Substage (4–10). Needs and key figure identifications are dominant.
2. Interest Substage (11–12). Likes are the major determinant of aspirations and activities.
3. Capacity Substage (13–14). Abilities are given more weight, and job requirements (including training) are considered.

II. **Exploration Stage (age 15–24)**
1. Tentative Substage (15–17). Needs, interests, capacities, values, and opportunities begin to be synthesized.
2. Transition (18–21). Reality considerations are given more weight.
3. Trial—crystallization (22–24).

III. **Establishment Stage (25–44)**
1. Trial—specification (25–30).
2. Stabilization (31–44). For most persons, these are the creative years.

IV. **Maintenance Stage (age 45–64)**

V. **Decline Stage (age 65 on)**
1. Deceleration Substage (65–70).
2. Retirement Substage (71 on).

SOURCE: Super et al. (1957, pp. 40–41), edited and slightly adapted.

graders in 5 eastern Massachusetts communities. The youngest was 12 years old and the oldest was 15. Their average Otis IQ was 107, with a range from 88 to 131. Their families were well scattered in socioeconomic status and fathers' occupations. One thing the subjects had in common was that all had received an 8th-grade group guidance treatment based on *You: Today and Tomorrow* (Katz 1958). The subjects were interviewed intensively at that time, and at 2-year intervals through early 1967, for a total of 6 interviews over 11 years. Contact with them in 1969 and 1980 was mainly by telephone and by correspondence.[1]

At the beginning, the subjects perhaps belonged in the Capacity Substage of the Growth Stage, in the Career Development Stages outlined in table 1.1. Or, it might be argued, their recent experience of the group guidance program had accelerated many of them into the Tentative Substage of the Exploration Stage. In either case, the subjects were in the Exploration Stage for most of the period of CDS, and were in the Tentative Substage for most of the first part of CDS, as reported in *Emerging Careers* (Gribbons and Lohnes 1968). We do believe in the progression of developmental stages and tasks described in table 1.1, but we also believe that the ages assigned are modal rather than governing.

1. All the subjects were Caucasian, which reflected the ethic composition of their cities in 1958.

During adolescence the requirements are for understanding of: (1) personal abilities and motives, (2) the general structure of career opportunities, (3) an assessment of personal potentialities, and (4) tentative decisions for a career future. These may be stated as needs for *information* and *planning*. The degree of fulfillment of these tasks determines the extent of vocational maturity at this stage of life. However, it is crucial for optimal maturation that these tentative decisions be taken in such a way as to maximize ability for the future. It is ability or adaptability to criteria for entrance to several or many career tree branches that is termed "multipotentiality." At the Tentative Stage, the most mature behavior is to know and value one's multipotentiality and to plan to enhance it.

Vocational Maturity Measurement

CPS and CDS attempted to measure attributes of vocational maturity and then relate the measurements to later educational and vocational adjustments. CDS scaled 8 traits in a syndrome termed Readiness for Vocational Planning (RVP) from the 8th-grade interview protocols, and again from the 10th-grade protocols. The resulting 8th and 10th RVP score profiles were then correlated with each other and with all other variables collected in the first 4 data collections, through 2 years beyond high school. The resulting network of relationships comprised the empirical base for *Emerging Careers* (Gribbons and Lohnes 1968). Table 1.2 describes the eight RVP traits.

The RVP profiles were found to be only moderately stable from 8th to 10th grade (over a 2½ year span). The stability displayed by the profiles was taken as evidence of *persistence* of the syndrome, while the kinds of change that developed were interpreted as descriptive of the *emergence* of vocational maturity. There was an increase in mean performance and a decrease in variability of performance on every trait over the 2½ year period. The correlations among the traits also decreased over the same period. The largest mean increases were for Factors in Curriculum Choice, Values, and Factors in Occupational Choice, in that order. The Interests scale showed the least mean increase. Factor analyses seemed to confirm the multidimensionality of the vocational maturity indicators.

The RVP profiles were found to be related to curriculum plans and placements at several periods of time, level of occupational preference, higher education plans and placements, occupational level and group placements 2 years out of high school, and judged success or failure of adjustment 2 years beyond high school. In these predictive validity studies, the 8th RVP substantially outperformed the 10th RVP, a mat-

Table 1.2. Eight Readiness for Vocational Planning (RVP) Scales

---

VARIABLE I. *Factors in Curriculum Choice*
Awareness of relevant factors, including one's abilities, interests, and values and their relation to curriculum choice; curricula available; courses within curricula; the relation of curriculum choice to occupational choice

VARIABLE II. *Factors in Occupational Choice*
Awareness of relevant factors, including abilities, interests, values; educational requirements for choice; relation of specific high school courses to choice; accuracy of description of occupation

VARIABLE III. *Verbalized Strengths and Weaknesses*
Ability to verbalize appropriately the relation of personal strengths and weaknesses to educational and vocational choices

VARIABLE IV. *Accuracy of Self-Appraisal*
Comparisons of subject's estimates of his general scholastic ability, verbal ability, and quantitative ability with his actual attainments on scholastic aptitude tests, English grades, and mathematics grades

VARIABLE V. *Evidence for Self-Rating*
Quality of evidence cited by subject in defense of her appraisal of her own abilities.

VARIABLE VI. *Interests*
Awareness of interests and their relation to occupational choices.

VARIABLE VII. *Values*
Awareness of values and their relation to occupational choices.

VARIABLE VIII. *Independence of Choice*
Extent of subject's willingness to take personal responsibility for his choices.

---

ter of surprise and concern to the authors. We decided that we simply had done a poor job of analyzing and collecting information about the contents of vocational maturity at the 10th-grade level. We had carried over the same questions and the same scoring scheme from the 8th- to the 10th-grade interviews, and these seemed to have been very appropriate for the 8th grade, but by the 10th grade too many of the subjects had lost interest in these issues. Critics of CDS have pointed to the fact that the 8th RVP scores were somewhat contaminated with intelligence (multiple $R^2 = .32$), while the 10th RVP were not, and have wondered whether the greater predictive validities claimed for the 8th RVP are not really due to this intelligence contamination, since intelligence is a well-known predictor of most of our criteria. Unfortunately, the asserted multidimensionality of vocational maturity led to such conspicuous consumption of degrees of freedom for a study with such small N (total sample size) that joint predictions from IQ and RVP could not be explored. In this report we retreat to a unidimensional scaling of vocational maturity from the 8th-grade protocols in order to recover sufficient degrees of freedom to permit joint predictions from sex, socioeconomic status of family, intelligence, and vocational maturity, and show that the 8th-grade vocational maturity measure did have useful complementary predictive validities.

Career Patterns

Consistent with the belief that the life history of vocational adjustments is more important than any single adjustment, and indeed that the meaning of the single event is created by its relation to the history, psychology has recently shifted its focus from vocational placement to career pattern. Career is conceived as the process of educational and vocational development, and pattern is the profile of scores on a career variable observed repeatedly over a long time span. Since development is usually continuous, whereas scientific observation of developmental variables is usually occasional, it might be said that career pattern is the sequence of occupancies of a process variable as its continuous path is monitored intermittently. Theoretically the developmental variable always has a value and is a continuous time series, but practically the variable is measured discretely as a series of periodic values. Four career variables that were subjected to pattern analysis in *Emerging Careers* (Gribbons and Lohnes 1968) were (1) transitional coping behaviors, (2) educational aspiration, (3) level of occupational aspiration, and (4) group of occupational aspiration. The method of analysis was to fit Markov chains in an attempt to describe the inherent lawfulness of the developmental variables.

Markov chains are the simplest kind of probability law that can be asserted for career patterns, if we assume as we must that good career variables are not random walks. The primary parameters of chains are probabilities, each of which is the probability of a step from state j of the variable at time t to state k at time $t + 1$. If there are n states or levels of the developmental variable, these primary parameters are arrayed in a table with n^2 cells, in which the n rows represent the states at time t (or, the *leaving* states) and the n columns represent the states at time $t + 1$ (or, the *arriving* states). Thus, the probability in row j and column k is the probability of arriving at state k if one is leaving state j. The probabilities on the diagonal of the table from the upper left corner to the lower right corner are probabilities for staying where one was over the time period. The basic assumption of the Markov chain model is that one such table of transition probabilities applies to all transitions, regardless of the value of t. The table is therefore called the "matrix of stationary transition probabilities," meaning that transition probabilities are stationary over time.

The assumption of stationarity is of course extremely unrealistic for longitudinal human development variables. However, mathematicians have derived remarkable properties of stationary Markov chains, so we are interested in the powerful analytical products that become available if we achieve even loose fits of our data to chains. Also, since chains are far more reasonable simple hypotheses for developmental processes than are random walks, we are interested in the best fitting chain as a null hypothesis against which to compare more elaborate models for data. The ways in which data misbehave under the best chain hypothesis may be quite instructive to us in our theory building.

Markov chain data analysis begins with computation of the observed transition frequencies for each type of transition and for each time interval. Table 1.3 illustrates the results of this data reduction for a CDS variable called "Transitional Coping Behaviors." This variable was produced from clinical ratings of pairs of interview protocols, where each rated pair was a "last" and "current" protocol for the same subject. For each CDS subject, his 1958 8th-grade protocol and his 1961 10th-grade protocol were judged together for the type of transitional coping behavior evidence. Then his 1961 10th-grade protocol and his 1963 12th-grade protocol were paired and yielded a rating. The resulting two scores determined which cell of Transition Matrix 1

Table 1.3. Markov Chain Analysis of Transitional Coping Behaviors

	(Total Sample, N = 10)	
Markov	*Coping Behaviors*	
Group 1:	foundering; stagnation	
Group 2:	trial, instrumentation; establishment	

Initial Probabilities
Group 1: .64   Group 2: .36

Transition Matrix 1 (1958/61–1961/63)
(frequencies in brackets)

	Group 1	1961/63	Group 2
Group 1	.63 (44)		.37 (26)
1958/61			
Group 2	.30 (11)		.70 (28)

Transition Matrix 2 (1961/63–1963/65)

	Group 1	1963/65	Group 2
Group 1	.66 (37)		.34 (19)
1961/63			
Group 2	.39 (21)		.61 (33)

(1958/61–1961/63) the subject was tallied in. For example, if his 1958 and 1961 protocol pairing was rated as Group 1 and his 1961 and 1963 protocol pairing was rated as Group 2, he was tallied as one of the 26 subjects in row 1 and column 2 of Matrix 1. These 26 people comprised 37% or a .37 proportion of all the subjects who were assigned to Group 1 on the 1958/61 rating. The other 63% remained in Group 1 on the 1961/63 rating. Next, for each subject the 1963 and 1965 (2 years beyond high school) protocol pair was rated, making Transition Matrix 2 (1961/63–1963/65) possible. Matrices 1 and 2 are the data matrices to which a Markov chain was then fitted.

Table 1.3 illustrates some noteworthy aspects of Markov chain fitting. First, it is desirable to keep small the number of states or levels of the process variable. We had clinical ratings of protocol pairs into Super's 5 coping behaviors, but since we did not want to have to fit 25 parameters into a model for data based on 110 subjects, we clustered the coping behaviors into a "good" and "bad" dichotomy. (Alternately, it is even more desirable to have a large number of subjects. If we had had 1,100 subjects, we would gladly have employed Markov variables with as many as 5 categories, although we consider that 7 states or levels is about as many as a chain variable should ever have because of the problems of perceiving and interpreting the details of matrices with more than 50 entries.) For this example, the dichotomous variable is perhaps both more reliable and more valid than the 5 categories, given the youthfulness of these subjects versus the conceptual exegesis of Super's theory of coping behaviors (Super 1963). Second, the absolute minimum number of time points (or stages) for which observations must be available, if a chain is to be fitted, is 3, so that 2 observed transition matrices may be computed. We have 3 sequential ratings involved in this example. Third, the row sum of proportions or probabilities in any transition matrix must be 1, since all subjects leaving state j must arrive in one of the n column states. Fourth, the distribution of subjects at the first observation is particularly interesting and is abstracted as a vector of Initial Probabilities. For this example, almost two-thirds of the subjects started with a "bad" rating for their coping during the first 2 years of the study. Fifth, transition matrices may be diagonal-dominated, as these are, meaning that each row has its largest probability or proportion in the diagonal element, so that the best bet for any subject is that he will remain at his present state or level at the next stage.

A Markov chain is fitted according to rules for a kind of averaging of the observed transition matrices. All the analytical procedures we used are spelled out in Kemeny and Snell (1960), and the statistical

Table 1.4. Stationary Transition Matrix

	Group 1	Group 2
Group 1	.643	.357
Group 2	.351	.649

Stationarity hypothesis $\chi^2_2 = .94$, $.75 > p > .50$
Order zero versus order one $\chi^2_1 = 18.4$, $p < .001$
Order one versus order two $\chi^2_2 = .66$, $.75 > p > .50$

Powers of Stationary Matrix for Total Sample Coping Behaviors
Second Power (1958/61 Coping to 1963/65)

1958/61	Group 1	.54	.46
	Group 2	.45	.55

Third Power (1958/61 Coping to 1965/67)

1958/61	Group 1	.51	.49
	Group 2	.48	.52

Limiting Matrix (Equilibrium at Fourth Power)

	Group 1	.500	.500
	Group 2	.500	.500

Mean First Passage Times (standard deviations in brackets)

	Group 1	Group 2
Group 1	2.0 (1.9)	2.8 (2.2)
Group 2	2.8 (2.3)	2.0 (1.9)

procedures for testing obtained fits may be found in Anderson and Goodman (1957). Table 1.4 presents the Stationary Transition Matrix fitted to our example and some additional analytical results. The stationary probabilities tell us that, if one is leaving Group 1 *at any time* in the history of the process, the odds are .64 of arriving again in Group 1 and .36 of arriving in Group 2 at the next observation time, or stage. If one is leaving Group 2 at any time, the odds are .35 of arriving in Group 1 and .65 of arriving in Group 2 at the next stage. Since Group 1 is "bad" coping adjustment and Group 2 is "good" coping adjustment, we are led to believe that about two-thirds of the population will retain either a good or a bad rating over any one interval linking two stages. We speak of a population because, strictly speaking, the stationary probabilities are parameters of a theory for some population based on data analysis for the CDS sample. We wish we had a random sample of a specified population, but of course we do not. We can only say that if we knew a population from which our subjects could be a random sample, then this would be our best estimate of stationary probabilities for that population, assuming stationarity of the process in that population. Theory building from nonrepresentative case studies is a very tenuous business and is strictly exploratory, never confirmatory.

The three chi-square tests are supposed to assure us that: (1) the sample data conform to the assumption of a stationary process in the population; (2) the random walk (order zero chain), for which the behavior of subjects on each transition would be strictly independent of their previous histories, may be rejected as a theory for the population described by this sample; and (3) the sample data conform to the assumption of one-stage "memory" for the process in the population, meaning that only the last or leaving state for the subject influences his probabilities of arriving in the various possible arriving states, and his history with the process prior to the last or leaving state is irrelevant. This assumption of very short memory for the process is one of the unrealistic aspects of Markov chains as models for human development. We caution ourselves and the reader that, for the first and third chi-square tests, the desired outcome is failure to reject the null hypothesis, so that the increased sample size that increases the power of the test (the chances of rejecting a false null hypothesis) contradicts our human need for publishable "fits."

What do we learn from this analysis about transitional coping behaviors during the Tentative Substage? We learn that there are approximately two chances out of three that a random 10th-grader will receive a negative rating for his 8th-to-10th grade transitional coping behavior, and two chances out of three that whatever rating he receives for this first two-year period will be repeated when the next two-year period is rated. If we have any faith in the clinical ratings, these trends are ominous. What do the data seem to portend for the future? The powers of the stationary matrix project the theory for the process variable into the future, one stage ahead for each integer step in power. When further powering does not change the entries, as occurs for this stationary matrix after the fourth power, the process is said to have reached equilibrium, after which the long-range prediction for all individuals is the same regardless of the states in which they originally entered the chain. In our example, the fourth power matrix, describing the theoretical probabilities for the long step from 1958/61 state to 1967/69 state is already the Limiting Matrix that characterizes the process in equilibrium. These particular limiting probabilities are disconcerting in that they project that before long half of the population will be relegated to bad coping ratings, and this unfortunate proportion in limbo will be maintained thereafter.

The Mean First Passage Times give the theory's projection of the average number of stages for each of the four types of transitions to occur, along with standard deviations. Thus, subjects leaving Group 1 would arrive back in Group 1 at the average rate of 2.0 stages. Since we know that two-thirds of the subjects will make the passage *from* Group 1 *to* Group 1 in one step, this average first passage time of two steps indicates that those among the one-third who do arrive at Group 2 in one step will be quite slow to return to Group 1. This is encouraging for those who "escape" from a bad leaving rating, but unfortunately the same slow rate of return applies to those who "slip" from a good leaving rating. (Note: the symmetry apparent in the matrices of this example is *not* a general property of Markov chain matrices.)

Testing Markov Chains

Tables 1.3 and 1.4 report a Markov chain analysis of the data CDS collected on coping behaviors in adolescence. Given our grave doubt about the chi-square tests of goodness of fit, how can we evaluate this chain theory for the coping process? The most rigorous test is to require the theory to predict future events. Table 1.5 reports two views of the predictive validity of the theory based on analyses of the next set of ratings, those from the pairing of the 1965 and the 1967 protocols. In 1967 the subjects were four years beyond high school. Some were already college seniors. The stationary transition matrix ought to describe the conditional distribution of transitions from 1963/65 ratings to the new 1965/67 ratings, if the process is stationary. The upper section of table 1.5 compares the theory probabilities with the actual propor-

Table 1.5. Test of Fit of Stationary Matrix against 1967 Observations

	Transition Matrix 3 (1963/65–1965/67)		
	Group 1	1965/67	**Group 2**
Group 1	Observed .57 (33)		Observed .43 (25)
1963/65	Expected .643 (37.3)		Expected .357 (20.7)
	$\chi^2 = .50$		$\chi^2 = .89$
Group 2	Observed .35 (18)		Observed .65 (34)
	Expected .351 (18.3)		Expected .649 (33.7)
	$\chi^2 = .01$		$\chi^2 = .00$

Goodness of fit hypothesis $\chi_2^2 = 1.40$, p ~ .50

	Test of Fit of Fourth Power of Stationary Matrix		
	against 1958/61 to 1965/67 Transitions		
	Group 1	1965/67	**Group 2**
Group 1	Observed .486 (34)		Observed .514 (36)
1958/61	Expected .500 (35)		Expected .500 (35)
	$\chi^2 = .03$		$\chi^2 = .03$
Group 2	Observed .450 (18)		Observed .550 (22)
	Expected .500 (20)		Expected .500 (20)
	$\chi^2 = .20$		$\chi^2 = .20$

Goodness of fit hypothesis $\chi_2^2 = .46$, .75 < p < .90

tions from the data. We see that slightly more escaped from Group 1 on this transition (.43) than predicted (.36), but the arrivals of those leaving Group 2 are exactly as predicted. We could not have a much better fit of data to theory.

The more difficult test for the theory is to predict the long-range outcomes conditional on where the subjects entered the chain in 1958/61 ratings. Technically, the third power of the stationary probabilities matrix gives the predictions for three-step outcomes, but, since the fourth power in this case is already the limiting matrix, we decided to derive our long-range predictions from it. The lower section of table 1.5 compares the actual long-step conditional distributions with those predicted from the equilibrium theory. We see one more person has escaped from Group 1 over the nine-year span than was predicted, whereas two fewer slipped from Group 2 than predicted. Altogether, this is a fairly tight-fitting theory.

One might ask whether all this tells us more about the behavior of the judges than about the coping of the subjects. Perhaps so, although we have some faith in the ratings, since we made them. We have been willing to consume this example to illustrate the Markov chain approach to data analysis because we have more convincing examples for later discussion. What we want to show here is how Markov chain analysis can fit a simple probability law to a discrete adjustment variable observed three or more times over a developmental span, and how the new data of the next observation point in the developmental process can be deployed to test the predictive validity of the fitted law. To the extent that the fit is tight, the process variable may be said to follow a simple law that is inherent in its own dynamics, and there would seem to be little need for external predictors of the variable. If the fit is loose or hopeless, one can either try to fit a more complicated type of probability law or search for external predictors for a statistical law. We are interested in the latter option. We hope to predict statistically from external, antecedent trait predictors the behavior of career pattern variables that are not entirely self-predicting. We have invented a scheme for combining internal chain predictability and external trait-statistical predictability that we will describe and illustrate. We believe all this has practical applications for the design of information systems for career guidance.

Discriminant Analysis

From the viewpoint of data analysis, the most salient feature of CDS is that its criterion or outcome variables have all been discrete, categorical, nominal, or ordinal classification measurements. The criteria have *not* been the continuously, normally distributed measurement scales that are required by the classical statistical prediction procedures of regression analysis. The reason for this is that career psychology is concerned with the determinants of plans, goals, choices, and decisions in the realms of education and vocation, and the natural language for expression and recording of plans, goals, choices, and decisions involves the syntax of categorization. People choose and decide in terms of elements from lists, ordered and unordered. Also, because people can juggle mentally only small numbers of elements simultaneously, long lists (e.g., the thousands of occupational titles or the hundreds of names of colleges and universities) naturally get sorted and collected into smaller categories (vocational groups or types of colleges). Since our research is intended to help young people plan and decide their career issues, it is appropriate that we formulate our criterion variables in rubrics that are natural and suitable for the decision making of such clients.

On the other hand, most of the predictors employed in career psychology are naturally conceived as continuously, normally distributed measurement scales. This is because the major investigations in the field of career development research have started with adolescent subjects and have accepted the existing adolescent personality as the primary basis for predicting future educational and vocational adjustments. It is to individual differences in adolescent personality that CPS, CDS, and TALENT have looked for predictor variables. Personality is considered to be the total repertoire of regular, persistent behavioral tendencies of an individual. It comprises almost the entire universe of action potentials for a person. The behavioral *trait* is the atom of this universe. The behavioral *factor* is the molecule combining these atoms, or traits. The trait is the element of behavior that the empiricism of objective psychology observes and records quantitatively; the factor is inferred from the data on traits as a constructed explanation of the observed variances and covariances of traits. The trait is measured directly by applying a scoring formula to a record of behaviors. The factor is measured by applying a scoring formula to the vector of scores on several traits. The factor is essentially the scientist's invention to simplify the network of information created by simultaneous measurement of many traits.

It is conventional and useful to classify behavioral traits and factors in a dichotomy of *abilities* and *motives,* defining abilities as what the person can do and motives as what he prefers to do. The distinction, we must remember, belongs to the technology of psychometrics, where maximum performance ability tests must be discussed separately from typical performance inventories. In the person who is the subject of investigation, personality is always a synthetic system in which all the traits are interlocked within one network of correlated behavioral tendencies. If we are to use the analogy of atom and molecule, we must be sure that our scientific psychology resembles biochemistry, not physical chemistry.

To clarify the relationship of career psychology to trait-and-factor psychology, it is helpful to distinguish *first phase longitudinal human development research* (FPLHDR)—which is concerned with the etiology of adolescent and adult individual differences in personality, and looks to genetic, child-rearing, peer group, and school variables as predictors of traits and factors of personality—from *second phase longitudinal human development research* (SPLHDR)—which is concerned with the consequences of individual differences, and uses traits and factors as predictors. Anne Roe and her students represent the sole example known to us of a career research program in the FPLHDR mode. Multiple regression procedures are usually ideal for FPLHDR. CDS and other programs of SPLHDR have had to look elsewhere than regression for data analysis procedures. What statistics does one use when the predictors are a syndrome of normally distributed traits or factors of personality and the criterion is a classification variable?

Under the leadership of Truman Lee Kelley in the 1930s and 1940s, the Harvard Graduate School of Education became a hotbed of inquiry and vision regarding vocational guidance. Kelley, himself an all-round statistician, psychometrician, and psychologist of individual differences—what we might term with some awe a "mighty traits-man"—collected around him a team of similarly inclined younger men who carried on the program after him. This coterie recognized that methodological problems were central to the ambitions they had for vocational development and guidance research. Lohnes (1966) has described Kelley's strong influence on the American practice of factor analysis. Kelley's successors at Harvard concentrated on the problem of statistical procedure for SPLHDR, evolving the multiple group discriminant analysis as a solution. The technical exposition of this strategy can be found in Rulon et al. (1967) and Cooley and Lohnes (1962). One of the pioneering applications is that of Tiedeman and Sternberg (1952), in which high school curriculum groups are discriminated in a measurement space based on the Differential Aptitudes Tests. Their paper is titled "Information Appropriate for Curriculum Guidance"! A large-scale application of discriminant strategy is provided by Cooley and Lohnes (1968), who relied upon this methodology for "Predicting Development of Young Adults," an extensive series of Project TALENT followup studies.

Discriminant analysis locates the weighted combinations of the predictor traits or factors that best separate the cells, groups, states, or levels of the classification criterion. When there are three or more cells in the criterion variable, there may be two or more linear functions, called "discriminant factors," required to describe fully the differences among the cells. These two or several discriminant factors may be conceptualized as uncorrelated factors of the predictor assessment that define a Cartesian subspace within the predictor measurement space in which group differences are best observed. Discriminant analysis is heuristic in that its primary purpose is to discover that subspace in which group differences are maximized. Inferential statistics of the analysis of variance sort are associated with the strategy, but the outcomes of data analysis are mostly descriptive. We learn which are the best factors of the personality assessment for separating the criterion groups, and we get a map of the locations of the groups in the space spanned by the discriminant, as well as information about the extent to which the groups overlap each other. We are also able to compute for any subject, from his score vector on the personality assessment, the relative probability of his membership in each of the groups. This last is an outcome obviously attractive for the guidance counseling game.

An example drawn from Cooley and Lohnes (1968) will not only illustrate the method; because the TALENT assessment of adolescent personality represented practically the complete state of the art, involving 60 ability traits and 38 motive traits, this example will also convey the best view we now have of which adolescent personality factors maximally discriminate vocational aspiration groups. As the first step in the research strategy, Lohnes (1966) transformed the 60 ability traits into a derived set of 13 factors, the names of which are reported in table 1.6. He argued that Verbal Knowledges make up a g-type intelligence factor; English and Mathematics are scholastic achievement factors; Visual Reasoning, Perceptual Speed and Accuracy, and Memory are differential aptitudes; and the others are special knowledge factors included to insure completeness of the factor solution. Lohnes also transformed the 38 motive traits into 13 factors, as named in table 1.6. Here, he argued, there are four interest factors—Business, Outdoor and Shop, Cultural, and Science; two activities factors—Scholasticism and Activity Level; two self-concept factors—Conformity Needs and Impulsion; and three lesser factors that again indicate completeness of factoring. The value of this a priori factoring of the enormous predictor battery of 98 traits is that it gives us a reasonably concise set of rubrics in terms of which to conceptualize adolescent personality. The original 98-atom assessment profiles of the

Table 1.6. Factors for Two TALENT Batteries

Mnemonic	Factor Name	Variance Extracted
	Abilities Domain Factors	
VKN	Verbal Knowledges	18.7%
GRD	Grade	7.8
ENG	English Language	6.6
SEX	Sex	5.7
VIS	Visual Reasoning	5.3
MAT	Mathematics	4.1
PSA	Perceptual Speed and Accuracy	3.6
SCR	Screening	3.3
H-F	Hunting-Fishing	2.2
MEM	Memory	2.1
COL	Color, Foods	1.9
ETI	Etiquette	1.6
GAM	Games	1.5
	(13 factors extract 64.6% of variance)	
	Motives Domain Factors	
CON	Conformity Needs	11.1%
SEX	Sex	9.1
BUS	Business Interests	8.7
OUT	Outdoors, Shop Interests	6.8
SCH	Scholasticism	6.6
CUL	Cultural Interests	5.8
SCI	Science Interests	4.3
GRD	Grade	4.2
ACT	Activity Level	4.0
LEA	Leadership	3.1
IMP	Impulsion	2.8
SOC	Sociability	2.8
INT	Introspection	2.4
	(13 factors extract 71.5% of variance)	

9,122 male TALENT subjects were transformed into the 22-molecule profiles before the discriminant analysis was computed. Thus the 12th-grade personalities of these youths are represented in this study by their 22 factor scores, which are termed MAP scores. The score vector for each youth represents a point in the 22-dimension MAP space. For this study, that point is the abstraction of the adolescent's personality. Science always deals with a less-than-real world.

The criterion variable was coded from the 5-year followup questionnaires and represents the career aspirations of the subjects at a point when they were 5 years beyond high school and 5 years after their personalities were assessed. Table 1.7 names the 12 categories into which the aspirations were grouped, along with the percentage of males 5 years beyond high school that was estimated by Project TAL-

Table 1.7. Twelve-Category Criterion for 1965 Followup
(five years out of high school; N = 14,799)

		Mnemonic
1. Ph.D. or M.D., Biological and Medical Sciences	1%	MED
2. D.D.S., M.S., or B.S., Biological and Medical Sciences	2	BIO
3. Ph.D., Physical Sciences and Mathematics	1	RES
4. M.S. or B.S., Physical Sciences and Engineering	8	ENG
5. Skilled and Technical Occupations with Post-High School Training	15	TEC
6. Laborers, No Post-High School Training	9	LBR
7. Clerks and Office Workers, No Post-High School Training	17	CLK
8. Noncollege, Nontechnical, with Post-High School Training	19	ACT
9. B.S. or B.A., Business	10	BUS
10. Graduate School, Business	1	MGT
11. B.S. or B.A., Sociocultural	12	WEL
12. Graduate School, Sociocultural	5	PRF

ENT to be in each aspiration group. (The rationale for this grouping is explained in the next section of this chapter.) For the moment, note that the criterion variable depends on both educational and vocational aspirations. It reflects both interest orientation and level of aspiration.

By analysis of variance F-ratios, the 22 MAP measures were ranked for strength of association between predictor and the classification criterion, and the means for the 12 groups on the 6 top-ranking measures appear in table 1.8. Scholasticism, a motive variable, had the largest F-ratio, followed by Mathematics and Verbal Knowledges, 2 abilities, with the 3 interests—Science, Outdoor and Shop,

Table 1.8. Group Means on Best MAP Predictors for 1965 5-Year Followup
Career Plans
(with Multiple Regression Coefficients for Factors)

Career Plans Group		N	Rank: 3 Factor VKN R^2 .44	2 MAT .54	1 SCH .54	5 OUT .33	6 CUL .29	4 SCI .41
1	MED	279	61	80	62	57	42	73
2	BIO	438	57	69	56	62	38	70
3	RES	221	61	84	63	60	38	72
4	ENG	939	56	74	57	64	35	69
5	TEC	1,297	50	59	49	67	35	61
6	LBR	706	46	54	46	69	34	56
7	CLK	530	49	53	48	64	37	58
8	ACT	1,430	53	57	49	63	38	60
9	BUS	1,214	56	65	54	61	36	65
10	MGT	270	60	75	59	57	36	68
11	WEL	1,183	57	64	54	60	43	64
12	PRF	815	61	72	59	57	44	66

and Cultural—coming next in ranking. Three abilities and 5 motives figure in the first 9 rank positions. The multiple R values may be read as correlation ratios between the MAP measures and the classification. These range from moderate (.54) to weak (.18). No single MAP measure is a strong predictor of the criterion. We see that the research scientists and medical doctors are highest on Verbal Knowledges, Mathematics, Scholasticism, and Science Interests. All the group centroids (profile of means) are convincing. (Note that the MAP factors were scaled to a population mean of 50 and a standard deviation of 10.) The ways in which the 4 interests differentiate groups with similar abilities are particularly noteworthy (e.g., B.A. Business and B.A. Sociocultural groups differentiated by the higher Cultural Interests of the latter).

Table 1.9. Factor-Discriminant Correlations and Canonical Correlations for 5-Year Followup Career Plans in 12th-Grade MAP Space

	Canonical Correlation	Discriminant Functions*		
		I	II	III
		.69	.37	.23
MAP Factors				
Abilities				
Verbal Knowledges		.62	.20	− .07
Perceptual Speed, Accuracy		.02	.10	− .17
Mathematics		.73	− .49	− .07
Hunting-Fishing		− .10	− .26	− .03
English		.28	.23	.06
Visual Reasoning		− 0.1	− .43	− .07
Color, Foods		.08	.10	.15
Etiquette		.05	.07	− .10
Memory		.00	.01	.05
Screening		− .33	− .25	.05
Games		.10	− .05	− .29
Motives				
Business Interests		− .04	.31	− .51
Conformity Needs		.21	.12	− .08
Scholasticism		.78	− .19	− .06
Outdoors, Shop Interests		− .41	− .42	.07
Cultural Interests		.25	.47	.61
Activity Level		− .22	− .10	− .10
Impulsion		− .01	.08	− 0.6
Science Interests		.54	− .36	− .23
Sociability		− .19	.47	− .43
Leadership		.28	.22	.04
Introspection		− .06	− .03	.18

*DF I: Science-oriented Scholasticism; DF II: Technical versus Sociocultural; DF III: Business versus Cultural.

Table 1.10. Discriminant Function Centroids for 1965 5-Year Followup Career
Plan Groups

Plan Group	DF I	DF II	DF III
1 MED	64	48	54
2 BIO	55	47	50
3 RES	62	41	52
4 ENG	54	44	48
5 TEC	43	46	51
6 LBR	38	48	53
7 CLK	41	52	50
8 ACT	45	53	49
9 BUS	52	52	46
10 MGT	59	51	45
11 WEL	53	54	52
12 PRF	59	54	53

Although 11 discriminant factors are possible in the analysis of 12 groups in 22-dimensional space, in fact only 3 useful discriminant factors were found, and these are described by their correlations with the 22 predictors, in table 1.9. The squared canonical correlations may be read as correlation ratios between the discriminant factors and the classification. Only the first canonical R^2 is substantial, but it shows a relation between the discriminant and the classification (.69) that is considerably higher than that of the best single predictor, Scholasticism, with the classification (.54). Cooley and Lohnes named the first function "Science-oriented Scholasticism," because of its strong correlations with SCH (.78), MAT (.73), VKN (.62), and SCI (.54). The second function, called "Technical versus Sociocultural," separates people who are strong on MAT and VIS abilities and OUT interest from those high on CUL and SOC. The third function separates high BUS and SOC people from high CUL people. One important aspect of this finding is that the best discriminant factors require contributions from both abilities and motives in their definitions; also important is the question of which abilities and which motives are heavily involved in the discrimination. Table 1.10 reports the centroids of the 12 groups in the 3 discriminant space, and Figure 1.1 plots the locations of the 12 groups in the plane of the best 2 discriminant factors. It is a very informative mapping of career aspiration groups in a personality plane. A lot of money and effort went into this trait-statistical assay of 9,000 lives. Can the findings be made available to young people in ways that will help them to think out their possible futures?

Discriminant analysis played the major data reduction role in the first part of CDS, and we now have a new series of such analyses to report, involving criteria from the interviews 4 years beyond high school (1967) and 6 years beyond high school (1969). Chapters 2 and 3

Figure 1.1 Centroids of Five-Year Followup Career Plan Groups in Discriminant Pl

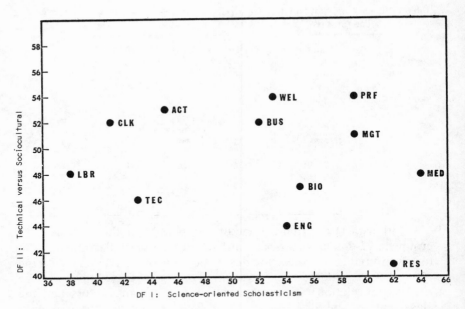

describe these studies. We do not have the detailed assessment of adolescent personality that TALENT has, but we are able to complement measures of intelligence with measures of sex, socioeconomic status of family, and vocational maturity as additional predictors of career adjustments in early adulthood.

Summary

The first 5-year phase of the Career Development Study (CDS) concentrated on indicators of vocational maturity, as hypothesized by Super, in its 8th- and 10th-grade interviews, conducted in 1958 and 1961 with the same 57 boys and 54 girls. The key indicators turned out to be information relevant to high school curriculum choice and a readiness to plan. There was evidence of continuity and progress in vocational maturity traits over the 2½ years, but it was also observed that some youths seemed to be better prepared for decision making in the 8th grade than others were in the 10th grade. The authors believe that many students were ill prepared for the forced choice of a high school curriculum.

Vocational maturity, especially as measured in the more successful 8th grade RVP scales, was found to be related to subsequent educational and vocational aspirations, plans, and choices during the high school years and in the 2 years immediately after high school. The 8th grade RVP scales were also related to judged success or failure in coping behaviors 2 years beyond high school.

Several career pattern variables were reduced to reasonably fitting Markov chains in a methodological probe that seemed promising for the future of the project. Discriminant analysis was shown to be an appropriate data analysis procedure for such second-phase longitudinal human development research as CDS, but it was apparent that a link-up of Markov chain and discriminant procedures should be developed.

Overall, life seemed to be grinding away at the idealism or fantasies of the young people during the Tentative Substage of Exploration. Early on there was obvious, extensive overaspiration. Gradually the aspirations for higher education and professional vocations eroded, and goals and expectations became more realistic.

2
Transition: Four Years Beyond High School

In 1958, W. D. Gribbons initiated the first stage of the longitudinal study described herein with a carefully selected sample of 111 junior high students. Personal interviews were conducted with the 57 boys and 54 girls, using an interview schedule designed to stimulate the youngsters to demonstrate their ability to analyze and synthesize facts about themselves and the world of work in making decisions for the future.[1] Basically, the complex and multidimensional interview schedule was concerned with aspects of the quality of planning done by youth. It was hypothesized that the scales based on the interview protocol would provide a basis for predictions of emerging career groupings and thus enrich the knowledge and theory of career development. Because so much rich and potentially valuable material was obtained in these interviews and from the school records, Gribbons applied for funds to continue study of the careers of these youngsters until they reached rather stable stages of their career development. Thus far, under funding from the U. S. Office of Education (Projects No. 5-0088 and No. 6-2151), the subjects have been interviewed every 2 years from grade 8 to 6 years out of high school, excepting only 3 subjects not reached in the period covered by this report. The results of the first phase of this project, which includes grade 8 to 2 years out of high school, are reported in detail in *Career*

1. This was the first of two interviews that attempted to evaluate the short-term effect of a group guidance unit, *You: Today and Tomorrow*, written by Martin Katz (1958) for the Guidance Inquiry of Educational Testing Service. This study was supported in part by the Rockefeller Brothers Fund and in part by Educational Testing Service, Princeton, New Jersey. Only the pre-*YT&T* interviews have been used in the Career Development Study.

Development (Gribbons and Lohnes 1966) and *Emerging Careers* (Gribbons and Lohnes 1968).

The longitudinal study of careers has had the following specific objectives:

1. Test the theory of occupational choice that proposes a process running through a sequence of developmental stages.
2. Determine whether there are significant sex differences in career sequences.
3. Describe in detail 110 real careers over 11 years of development, and seek unifying mathematical and psychological models for them.
4. Determine the extent to which career decisions are based upon selected self-concept and other factors, answering such questions as:
   What is the role of intelligence in choosing, entering, and remaining in an occupation?
   What is the role of values in making choices?
   What is the impact of value shifts as they occur with maturation?
   What effects do familial and societal pressures have in shaping occupational aspiration?
5. Accomplish a successful multidimensional scaling of early vocational maturing from an interview protocol, naming the resulting scales, as a set, Readiness for Vocational Planning (RVP).
6. Explore the statistical dependence of numerous criteria of career development on the RVP scales, collecting the criteria in followup interviews every two years for a total of 11 years.

It was recognized from the outset that the use of a personal interview and a longitudinal design would limit the number of subjects we could include in the study, but it is our judgment that the followup personal interview produced data of a quality and completeness that could not be matched using any other research design. The rapport generated by the interview not only preserved contact with all subjects from grade 8 to 2 years out of high school, and a loss of only 3 subjects in the 6 years out of high school collection, but it seems to have encouraged a sincerity of responses that questionnaires do not evoke. Therefore, we continued with this design as the best available method for reaching the objectives. In addition to the personal interviews, however, at 4 years out of high school all subjects completed a number of questionnaires and inventories.

Although it was not possible to achieve a random sample of communities for this investigation, comparisons of characteristics of the five Massachusetts communities in the sample—Beverly, Newton, Revere, Somerville, and Stoneham—with other urban communities in the U.S. indicated that, in most respects examined (e.g., Trends in Population, Distribution of Population by Age, Educational Level of Persons 25 Years and Over, Civilian Labor Force, Employed Personnel Classified into Occupational Groups, and Income in 1949), the sample cities as a whole do not differ greatly from national trends.

The 57 boys and 54 girls included in the study were selected from 9 classrooms in the 5 cities by means of a random numbers table. The mean IQ of the group as measured by the Otis Test, Beta Form, was 107 with a range from 88 to 131. The ages, in the 8th grade, ranged from 144 months to 190 months with an average age of 160 months. Socioeconomic status, rated by Hamburger's revision of Warner's scale (1958), indicated that all major occupational groups were included among the parents of students in the sample, and the occupations tended to fall at the middle of the scale.

It was recognized that the inclusion of both sexes in a sample of this size involved some risks, but careful consideration suggested it would be worthwhile. Up to that time, little or no attention had been given to the career development of girls. Do they also go through developmental stages? If they do, are their stages similar to the stages delineated for boys? If they differ, how effective is their counseling when boys and girls are not treated differently?

The main technique for gathering data has been standardized personal interviews with each subject. The interview schedule, which was modified as changes became necessary, was devised in a pilot study before use with this group. (A complete set of interviews and scoring manuals used from grade 8 to high school plus 2 years can be found in *Career Development* (Gribbons and Lohnes 1966). Most of the questions were designed to stimulate the pupils to reveal their thinking processes in making choices and to demonstrate their ability to analyze and synthesize information about themselves and the educational and vocational worlds.

A review of instruments used by other researchers, particularly those of Super's Career Pattern Study and Project TALENT, resulted in the selection of a number of questionnaires and scales that were administered to each subject when applicable. In choosing the particular instruments to be used, it was necessary to consider the amount of time we could reasonably expect from our subjects without losing rapport or their interest, as well as the amount of useful information a sample of this size could supply. A short description of the HS + 4 (high school plus 4 years) instruments follows.

HS + 4 Instruments

Personal Interviews. Seventy-eight questions designed to obtain in some depth the subjects' attitudes toward work, education, and homemaking, and their satisfaction with work and life in general. Subject is given opportunity to demonstrate his thinking processes in making vocational and educational decisions. For the most part these responses will be used as criterion data and correlated with data obtained from earlier personal interviews.

N = 105
Time required: 1 to 2 hours

Interest Inventory—Project TALENT. Designed to measure the relative interests in occupations, which range from bookkeeping to U.S. Senator. Subject indicates his degree of interest in each of 122 occupations. These findings will be related to earlier stated interests of subjects and to 8th- and 10th-grade Readiness for Vocational Planning (RVP) scores.

N = 106
Time required: Approx. 10–15 minutes

Activities Inventory—Project TALENT Personality Test. Answers will help to add to knowledge of how personality differences account for the differences in accomplishment of equally talented normal people.

N = 106
Time required: Approx. 10–15 minutes

Occupational Aspirations Scale and Work Beliefs Inventory (Haller and Miller, Michigan State University). Designed to determine both realistic and idealistic expressions of level of occupational aspirations as well as attitudes toward and beliefs about work. Subject's level of occupational aspirations can be compared with that of the subject's peers and correlated with RVP scores and IQ and socioeconomic status.

N = 106
Time required: Approx. 20 minutes

Job Master Form—Career Pattern Study. Subject details job experience, rates satisfaction in many facets of job, and general feelings of success with present job. Data will be correlated with data collected in earlier interviews.

N = 91
Time required: Approx. 20 minutes

Military Form—Career Pattern Study. Subject details past and present military status, training experiences, and his evaluation of success and satisfaction with military experiences. Responses will be correlated with earlier responses, especially 8th- and 10th-grade RVP scores.

N = 19
Time required: Approx. 20 minutes

Training and Education Form—Career Pattern Study. Details past and present educational status, success, and satisfaction in various aspects of training/education programs. Data will be correlated with data collected in earlier interviews.

N = 60
Time required: Approx. 20 minutes

Our initial HS + 4 contacts were telephone calls to the subjects' homes or other places they had suggested in previous meetings to ascertain that our addresses and names, in the case of married women, were correct. Only one parent refused to give her son's military address or to forward our letter to him. The next step was to mail to each subject an individually typed letter requesting a meeting, an appointment form to be filled out, and a self-addressed, stamped envelope. Of the 110 living subjects, 70 responded to the first request, 31 required a followup registered letter and/or a telephone call, and several letters or telephone calls were required for 5 subjects. These efforts resulted in the completion of 92 personal interviews and 14 mailed questionnaires.

In order to hold the interviewer variable at a minimum, 2 interviewers conducted the personal interviews; 64 were interviewed at Regis College, 23 were interviewed at the subjects' homes in the Metropolitan Boston area, and 5 subjects were interviewed within a 250-mile radius of the Boston area.

Status of Subjects at HS + 4 Years

Table 2.1 displays for each subject his or her actual HS + 4 educational and occupational status, and his occupational and educational aspirations. (Similar listings for grade 8 to HS + 2 are contained in *Career Development* [Gribbons and Lohnes 1966]). For most of the subjects, present occupational status can be classified within a few general categories: 25 students, 16 military personnel, 27 clerk-secretaries, and 14 housewives. Thus 82 of 109[2] subjects are found within 4 occupational categories. As would be expected, particularly with so many students and military personnel, a much wider range of occupations is noted when one considers aspirations. Twenty men aspire to occupations in the business-managerial area, 11 aspire to professionally oriented occupations, 9 contemplate jobs in the technical-skilled categories, 4 aspire to protective occupations, and the remaining 11 cover a wide variety of nonprofessional occupations. As will be noted in table 2.1, most of the women aspire to careers as housewives. Of the 34 aspiring housewives, however, 22 also contemplate occupations outside the home on a part-time basis or when the children are in school. Eight women aspire to professionally oriented occupations.

An examination of the actual education attained at HS + 4 indicates that 73 subjects are or have been involved in some post-high school education or training. Of this number, 36 have completed 1 year, 11 subjects 2 years, 11 subjects 3 years, and 15 were completing their 4th year of college. Thirty others graduated from high school, and 4 have completed from 8 to 11 years of schooling.

Table 2.1 also lists the educational aspirations of the group and indicates a larger number of males than females continuing to aspire to higher education. It must be noted, however, that this table does not reflect the 3 women who have already completed 2- or 3-year training programs and have, therefore, achieved their goals.

Table 2.2 compares actual HS + 4 status and aspirations for Roe Level and Group. When the men's actual positions are compared with their verbalized occupational preferences, it is apparent that there is an upward trend in Group 3 and a downward trend in Group 4. When Levels are examined, an upward surge is noted in Level 2, and a decrease is noted in Level 4. All Groups (except 9, the student category) are represented in the *aspiration* column, indicating a much wider spread than is evident in the *actual* column.

2. Although only 106 subjects were interviewed, current status information was available for 109 subjects.

Table 2.1. High School + 4 Years Actual Occupations and Occupational and
Educational Aspirations

Code	E*	Actual Occupation	Occupational Males Aspirations	Educational Aspirations
001	1	Military	Police Detective	Police Academy
002	0	Military	Business Field	College
003	4	Student	Bus. Management	Grad. School
004	3	Student	Law	Law School
005	2	Salesman	Gemologist	College
006	1	Salesman	Salesman	None
007	4	Student	Corp. President	Law School
008	4	Student	Banking	Grad. School
015	1	Military	Criminologist	Grad. School
016	1	Computer Operator	Computer Programmer	College
017	0	Clerk	Own Garage	None
018	3	Student	Psychologist	Grad. School
019	1	Student	Own Business	Law School
020	0	Military	Printer	Technical Courses
021	0	Bank Teller	Fire Dept.	None
028	0	Clerk (Pkg. Sorter)	Personnel Work	College
029	4	Student	Teacher	Law School
030	1	Military	None	College
031	2	Clerk (Pkg. Sorter)	Teacher	College
032	4	Student	Dentist	Grad. School
033	4	Student	Exec. Management	Grad. School
040	1	Military	Bus. Administration	College
041	3	Student	Teacher (Phys. Ed.)	Grad. School
042	1	Military	Flight Management	Airlines School
043	2	Student	Marketing	College
050	1	Military	Electronic Engineer	College
051	0	Shipper	Shipper	None
052	1	Draftsman	Draftsman	2 Yr. College
053	1	Bank Clerk	Accountant	Crses. in Acctng.
054	1	Military	Programmer	IBM Courses
055	2	Student	Journalism	College
056	1	Bank Teller	Bank Vice Pres.	None
057	2	Military	Movie Photographer	College
064	0	Musician	Tradesman	None
065	1	Machine Operator	Computer Dept. Super.	Vocational Courses
066	1	Military	Machinist	Vocational Courses
067	4	Student	Teacher	Grad. School
068	1	Salesman	Buyer	None
069	0	Salesman	Pub. Co. Exec.	Misc. Courses
076	0	Research Technician	Bank President	Misc. Courses
077	1	Insur. Accntng. Clk.	Accountant	College
078	0	Military		
079	1	Military	Science Field	College
080	1	Production Operator	Electronic Technician	Vocational Courses
081	0	Factory Worker	Crane Operator	None

Table 2.1. (Cont'd)

090	0	Owner, Fuel Oil Bus.	Auto Repair Business	Vocational Courses
092	1	Military	Bus. Management	College
093	3	Student	Bus. Mgmt./Law	Grad. School
095	0	Gas Station Attendnt.	Fire Dept. Captain	Misc. Courses
096	3	Salesman	Electronic Engineer	College
099	2	Student	Electronic Techcn.	2 Year College
100	4	Student	Electronic Engineer	Grad. School
102	4	Student	Business Executive	College & Trng. Program
104	1	Military	Personnel Mngmt.	Unspecified Schooling
106	4	Student	Pharmacology	Grad. School
108	1	Military	Electronic Techcn.	None
110		Deceased		

Females

009	4	Student	Hsewfe./Business	Grad. School
010	4	Student	Hsewfe./Teacher	College
011	2	Office Clerk	Social Worker	College
012	4	Student	Hsewfe./Counselor	College
013	2	Housewife	Housewife	None
014	2	Jr. Accountant	Social Worker	Grad. School
022	0	Clerk	Clerk	None
023	0	Housewife	Housewife	None
024	0	Teletype Operator	Jr. Secretary	Misc. Hobby Crses.
025	1	Secretary	Hsewfe./Secretary	Misc. Crses.
026	0	Sr. Clerk/Steno	Housewife	None
034	3	Hsewfe./Nurse	Nurse Supervisor	Misc. Crses.
035	0	Housewife	Hsewfe./Clerk	Misc. Crses.
036	1	Secretary	Housewife	None
037	3	Student	Foreign Service	Grad. School
038	3	Student	Secretary	Misc. Crses.
039	4	Student	Teacher	Grad. School
044	1	Bank Teller	Hsewfe./Asst. Mgr.	None
045	3	Dental Hygienist	Hsewfe./Dent. Hyg.	College
046	1	Housewife	Housewife	Misc. Crses.
047	1	Housewife	Housewife	College
048	2	Housewife	Hsewfe./Exec. Sec.	None
049	0	Clerk-Typist	Sec./Hsewfe.	Misc. Crses.
058	0	Housewife	Hsewfe./Med. Sec.	Vocational Crses.
059	0	Clerk/Housewife	Housewife	None
060	1	Lab. Technician	Funeral Director	Embalming School
061	0	Unemployed		
062	1	Singer	Hsewfe./Sales	Vocational Crses.
063	1	Dental Assistant	Hsewfe./D.Asst.	Misc. Crses.
070	0	Clerk	Accountant	Accounting Crses.
071	0	Clerk/Housewife	Housewife	None
072	0	Clerk/Housewife	Hairdresser/Hsewfe.	vocational Crses.

Table 2.1. (Cont'd)

	E			
073	0	Clerk/Housewife	Computer Programmer/ Housewife	Vocational Crses.
074	0	Housewife	Hsewfe./Office Wk.	High School Crses.
075	0	Housewife	Hsewfe./LPN†	LPN Training
082	0	Housewife/Nurse's Aide	Hsewfe./LPN	LPN Training
083	0	Production Operator	Housewife	None
084	1	Secretary/Housewife	Housewife	Misc. Courses
085	1	Legal Secretary	Hsewfe./Sec.	None
086	1	Housewife	Hsewfe./LPN	LPN Training
087	0	Housewife	Housewife	None
088	1	Clerk	Clerk	None
089	3	Nurse	Nurse/Hsewfe.	None
091	0	Clerk/Housewife	Hsewfe./Sec.	None
094	0	Secretary	Housewife	Misc. Courses
097	3	Nurse	Hsewfe./Nurse	College
098	4	Student	Teacher	Grad. School
101	0	Clerk/Housewife	Hsewfe./Tailor	Vocational Crses.
103	1	Nurse's Aid/Hsewfe.	Hsewfe./Nurse	Nursing School
105	0	Clerk/Housewife	Receptionist/ Housewife	None
107	2	Clerk	Housewife	None
109	1	Ballet Dancer	Dancer	Dance Lessons
111	0	Housewife/Waitress	Hsewfe./Leg. Sec.	Misc. Courses

*E = Actual educational level; 0 = HS or less; 1 = 1 yr. post HS; 2 = 2 yrs. post HS; 3 = 3 yrs. post HS; 4 = 4 yrs. post HS.
†Licensed Practical Nurse

When the women's actual positions are compared with their aspirations, however, one notes a decrease in Group 3 and an increase in Group 0; and an increase in Level 4 and a decrease in Level 5.

Actual HS + 4 occupations and occupation aspirations were rated according to Hamburger's revision of Warner's scale. An examination of table 2.3 shows that, with the exception of Level 7, there is a good distribution of subjects across socioeconomic levels. The preponderance of males at Level 1 can be accounted for by the male students who are presently enrolled in college. The high percentage of women at Level 5 is due to housewives (an arbitrary classification because Hamburger does not include housewives) and clerical occupations. Levels 2 and 3 show marked increases from actual occupations to aspirations, indicating a desire to move upward in the level of occupation.

Another way of examining mobility is to compare the subject's occupational preference at HS + 4 with his father's occupation, both of which have been rated on the Hamburger scale. Without regard to

Table 2.2. Roe Level and Group for High School + 4 Years
(Occupations: Actual and Aspirations)

Roe Group	Men Actual	Men Aspiration	Women Actual	Women Aspiration	Roe Level	Men Actual	Men Aspiration	Women Actual	Women Aspiration
0	0	1	15	34	0	0	0	0	0
1	0	3	0	1	1	0	4	0	0
2	0	3	0	3	2	19	32	9	8
3	16	25	22	7	3	7	9	5	3
4	20	11	1	1	4	17	6	21	38
5	0	1	0	0	5	10	3	15	3
6	1	4	6	3	6	3	0	2	0
7	0	6	0	2	7	0	1	1	0
8	1	1	2	1		56	55	53	52
9	18	0	7	0					
	56	55	53	52					

Roe Occupational Groups

0 Unemployed, No aspirations, Hsewfe.
1 Physical
2 Social and Personal Service
3 Business
4 Industry and Government
5 Math and Physical Sciences
6 Biological and Medical sciences
7 Education and Humanities
8 Arts
9 Student

Roe Occupational Levels

1 High Professional Managerial
2 Professional and Managerial
3 Semiprofessional and Low Managerial
4 Skilled Support and Maintenance
5 Semiskilled Support and Maintenance
6 Unskilled Support and Maintenance
7 Unemployed, No aspiration

sign, the subject's score was subtracted from the father's score, resulting in a discrepancy score. Table 2.4 indicates that 64 of the 106 subjects are found in the 0 and 1 categories, indicating a slight discrepancy, or none. The remaining 42 subjects had discrepancy scores of 2 or more SES levels. Although not shown in the table, it is interesting to note that, when signs were considered, only 24 aspired to occupations lower than their fathers', and 15 of these were girls who aspired to clerical-sales or housewife. The tendency of the group as a whole is toward upward mobility.

The sample has been geographically stable: 83 of the subjects continue to residence in their original towns, 16 have moved elsewhere in Massachusetts, and 10 have moved out of state.

Thirty-nine subjects have married, 16 males and 23 females; and there have been 4 divorces, 1 male and 3 females. Eleven of the subjects were engaged to be married in the near future.

The actual status of the group four years out of high school indi-

Table 2.3. HS + 4 Socioeconomic Status: Actual and Aspiration*

| | Actual Occupation | | | | Occupational Aspiration | | |
SES	Male	Female	Total	SES	Male	Female	Total
1	14	4	18	1	13	0	13
2	3	3	6	2	12	9	21
3	2	5	7	3	5	11	16
4	13	11	24	4	7	9	16
5	2	28	30	5	1	23	24
6	6	1	7	6	2	0	2
7	0	1	1				

*Military men have been omitted from this analysis.
NOTE: Students actual occupations rated on educational aspirations: i.e.; if stated
    graduate school, rated 1. Women: if full-time housewife rated 5; if worked,
    the occupation was rated. Aspirations for women: if aspired to occupation in
    future, the occupation was rated; otherwise rated as housewife.

cates that it is confined to rather narrow occupational categories, but in
terms of aspirations the group spreads out to cover most of the major
occupational categories. Also apparent in terms of Roe Level and SES
status is the desire for upward mobility.

Correlates of Educational Aspirations

In this section we will deal with some of the forces that affect the
young people as they meet and deal with vocational decisions in the
career development process. Curriculum, intelligence, socioeconomic
level, place of residence, and military service will be examined to
determine their relationships to the educational aspirations elicited
from our subjects at the time of each of the five interviews over the
nine-year period.

Educational Aspirations

It is clear from table 2.5 that there is a definite downward trend for
the total group over the nine years, with a sharper decrease noted for

Table 2.4. Socioeconomic Mobility

Discrepancy*	Frequency
0	22
1	42
2	22
3	14
4	4
5	2

*Discrepancy score is the difference between the Hamburger scale rating of the
subject's HS + 4 occupational preference and the father's occupation.

Table 2.5. Educational Aspirations
(8th, 10th, 12th Grade, HS + 2, and HS + 4 Frequencies)

Aspiration	8th Grade			10th Grade			12th Grade		
	M	F	Total	M	F	Total	M	F	Total
College	42	22	64	34	18	52	31	15	46
3 years	1	6	7	5	6	11	1	4	5
2 years	6	12	18	10	22	32	12	15	27
High School or less	8	14	22	8	8	16	13	20	33

Aspiration	HS + 2			HS + 4		
	M	F	Total	M	F	Total
College	33	17	50	31	11	42
3 years	5	1	6	0	1	1
2 years	10	15	25	15*	23*	38
High School or less	9	21	30	9	17	26

*Includes 1–2 years.

the girls (50%) than for the boys (26%). It is also clear that the percentage of boys aspiring to college far exceeds the percentage of girls aspiring to college.

The increase in the HS + 2 year category is inflated by the many subjects who said they intended to take a course or two but had no particular educational goal in mind.

Table 2.6. 8th- and 12th-Grade Curriculum vs. Actual Education at HS + 4*

	HS + 4 Actual Education											
	4 years of college				3 years of college				2 years of college			
Curriculum	M		F		M		F		M		F	
College	9	(9)	5	(5)	4	(4)	5	(5)	6	(6)	3	(4)
Business	0	(0)	0	(0)	0	(0)	0	(0)	0	(0)	0	(1)
I.A.† & Gen'l	0	(1)	0	(0)	0	(1)	0	(0)	0	(0)	0	(0)
Don't Know	1	(0)	1	(0)	1	(0)	0	(0)	0	(0)	2	(0)
Drop Out												

	1 year of college				High School Only				Total			
	M		F		M		F		M		F	
College	15	(9)	7	(7)	3	(5)	12	(1)	37	(33)	31	(22)
Business	2	(4)	8	(5)	7	(2)	7	(21)	9	(6)	16	(28)
I.A. & Gen'l	0	(4)	0	(1)	0	(2)	1	(1)	0	(8)	1	(2)
Don't Know	1	(0)	0	(0)	2	(0)	0	(0)	5	(0)	3	(0)
Drop Out					1	(3)	0	(2)	1	(3)	0	(2)

*Eighth-grade curriculum outside brackets, 12th-grade curriculum within brackets.
†

Curriculum Election

An examination of table 2.6 indicates that 14 of the 15 subjects presently enrolled in the 4th year of college were enrolled in the college preparatory curriculum in the 12th grade, and that 13 of the 15 stated preferences for that curriculum at the 8th grade. Of the 8 other students who are in varying stages of completing 4-year programs, 4 consistently chose college preparatory, and the remaining 4 alternated between college preparatory and the other curriculums. In addition, of the 22 students presently included in the 2–3 year category, 18 chose college preparatory in grade 8, and 19 were actually enrolled in that curriculum in grade 12. To some extent then, these data support Ginzberg's theory that occupational choice is an irreversible process, i.e., only 1 of our subjects was able to overcome the handicap of being in the "wrong" curriculum at grade 12. However, the reverse does not obtain: Many college preparatory subjects did not enter college, and this choice of curriculum did not prevent them from entering other fields that require less than a 4-year program. We feel that the educational system, which forces a youngster to commit himself to a curriculum choice at grade 8 or 9, has the responsibility of insuring that the youngster is ready and able to make this decision, and that, insofar as possible, it will encourage him to choose whichever curriculum will give him the greatest freedom of choice in the future. (Perhaps this means that almost all students should take a college preparatory curriculum.)

Intelligence

When the relationship between intelligence and level of educational aspirations (table 2.7) over the nine-year period is studied, it is interesting to note that both sexes in the 121 Plus IQ college aspirants demonstrate extremely high consistency. The shift to No Plans is accounted for by 3 women who are married, 1 woman who completed a 3-year nursing course, and 1 man in the military who anticipated taking a "few courses."

The 111–120 IQ group demonstrates a marked lowering (16 to 8) of aspirations from grade 8 to HS + 4, but a strong consistency of aspirations between grade 12 and HS + 4. The 101–105 and the 106–110 groups are much more consistent than the 100-and-Below group, which showed a rather dramatic drop from 13 subjects aspiring to college at grade 8 to 2 aspiring to college at HS + 4. This lowering of educational aspirations would seem to be a move in the direction of more realistic aspirations, but the loss of 17 subjects with college aspirations in the

Table 2.7. Educational Aspirations and IQ Group Frequencies

IQ Range	Educational Plans	Eighth Grade		Tenth Grade	
		M	F	M	F
100 and Below	College	7	6	7	3
	2–3 Years	3	2	3	6
	No Plans	4	3	4	2
101–105	College	8	2	7	2
	2–3 Years	2	5	4	6
	No Plans	2	3	1	2
106–110	College	10	2	6	1
	2–3 Years	1	7	4	10
	No Plans	1	3	2	1
111–120	College	9	7	7	5
	2–3 Years	1	1	2	5
	No Plans	0	4	1	2
121 Plus	College	8	5	7	7
	2–3 Years	0	3	2	1
	No Plans	1	1	0	1

IQ Range	Educational Plans	Twelfth Grade		HS + 2		HS + 4	
		M	F	M	F	M	F
100 and Below	College	7	1	4	2	1	1
	2–3 Years	1	5	6	4	2	0
	No Plans	6	5	4	4	10	10
101–105	College	5	3	8	3	8	2
	2–3 Years	6	3	2	2	0	1
	No Plans	1	4	2	5	4	7
106–110	College	6	1	7	1	8	1
	2–3 Years	2	3	4	4	0	0
	No Plans	4	8	1	7	4	10
111–120	College	6	3	7	5	6	2
	2–3 Years	3	7	3	4	0	0
	No Plans	1	2	0	3	3	9
121 Plus	College	7	7	7	6	8	5
	2–3 Years	1	1	0	1	0	0
	No Plans	1	1	2	2	1	4

111–120 and the 121 Plus groups would seem to be a loss to the body of college-trained manpower. It seems that, although intelligence has a relationship to consistency, it cannot account for the educational aspirations of many of our subjects.

Socioeconomic Level

When socioeconomic status (SES) was rated by Hamburger's revision of Warner's scale, all major occupational groups were found to

Table 2.8. Socioeconomic Status and Educational Aspirations at HS + 4
(8th-grade curriculum outside brackets; 12th-grade curriculum within brackets)

			Curriculum					
	College		2–3 years		1 year		HS or less	
SES	M	F	M	F	M	F	M	F
1	9 (9)	3 (2)	0 (0)	1 (0)	0 (0)	0 (0)	0 (0)	1 (2)
2	4 (3)	2 (1)	1 (0)	2 (0)	0 (2)	0 (3)	0 (0)	0 (0)
3	3 (3)	6 (3)	1 (0)	3 (0)	0 (1)	0 (2)	0 (0)	1 (4)
4	16 (8)	5 (3)	2 (2)	4 (1)	0 (6)	0 (1)	2 (2)	2 (4)
5	6 (5)	3 (0)	2 (0)	4 (0)	0 (1)	0 (6)	2 (3)	3 (4)
6	4 (2)	3 (1)	1 (0)	4 (0)	0 (1)	0 (6)	3 (3)	6 (3)
7			0 (0)	1 (0)	0 (1)	0 (0)	1 (0)	0 (1)

be included among the parents of the students—from Level 1 (high level) to Level 6 (lowest level)—and the occupations tended to fall at the middle of the scale. Table 2.8 reveals a positive relationship between high-level socioeconomic status and college aspirations—15 of 18 members of Level 1 consistently aspired to college—and a tendency for boys to have higher aspirations than do the girls. The remaining levels all showed a decrease in educational aspirations. Level 4 has the most marked drop with 8 of 16 boys and 2 of 5 girls lowering their aspirations.

An examination of intelligence test scores and SES levels (table 2.9) indicates that, with the exception of Level 6, the average IQ of the college aspirants is consistently higher than that of the nonaspirants. This would support the position that intelligence is an important factor in determining those who will aspire to college. However, when SES Levels 5 and 6 for nonaspirants are examined, it is found that the 11 subjects in these 2 classes have an average IQ of 100 (range 91–123), indicating that, although at least half of this group might be expected to have a chance of success in college, all have lowered their aspirations

Table 2.9. IQ and HS + 4 Educational Aspirations
(Eighth-grade aspirations outside brackets; 12th-grade within brackets)

	Educational Aspirations					
	Aspirants to College			Noncollege Aspirants		
SES	M	W	Av. IQ	M	W	Av. IQ
1	9 (9)	3 (2)	114	0	2	91
2	4 (3)	2 (1)	112	1	0	103
3	3 (3)	6 (3)	117	0	3	112
4	16 (8)	5 (3)	109	7	1	99
5	6 (4)	3 (0)	111	2	3	108
6	4 (2)	3 (0)	102	2	4	111

dramatically from grade 8 to HS + 4. In addition to this group, we find that 10 of the 17 subjects in the 111 Plus IQ group who also lowered their aspirations are from Levels 4, 5, and 6; 5 are from Level 3, and there is 1 each from Levels 1 and 2. How does this group of noncollege aspirants compare with the 111-Plus college aspirants? Fifteen of the 21 college aspirants are in Levels 1, 2, or 3; 4 are in Level 4; and 2 are in Level 2. These data suggest that socioeconomic level does indeed influence whether a young person will persist in aspirations for higher education, and we feel that it is not unreasonable to question whether more effective counseling could be instrumental in helping youngsters in the lower socioeconomic groups to realize their ambitions by giving them the extra incentive and information (e.g., work programs, scholarships, loans, etc.) they may not be receiving at home.

Place of Residence

Hamburger's classifications were used again to investigate the question of whether place of residence has any effect on aspiring and fulfilling aspirations to higher levels of education.

Examination of table 2.10 reveals that towns A and B fall into the lower half of the SES (using 3.5 as the dividing point), C and E fall into the upper half, and D has 1 school in the lower half and 1 school in the upper half of the scale. It is quite apparent that the number of college aspirants at grades 8 and 12 is far greater in the upper SES towns; and an even wider disparity is noted when one examines the actual educational level attained in HS + 4. It is, of course, impossible to attribute these results to any one particular environmental force, but it does seem that SES status of both the family and the place of residence play some part in determining the aspirations of the products of these families and towns.

Military Service

Nineteen of our male subjects (no information on 1 serviceman) have served or are serving in the armed forces. Some interesting trends are noted when we compare their educational aspirations at grade 12 with those at HS + 4. Nine of the men raised their aspirations during this period (6 to college), 3 lowered their sights—seemingly realistically because of IQs of 98, 97, and 111—and 6 remained unchanged. Of the 6 who remained constant, 4 were college-bound. These raised aspira-

Table 2.10. 8th- and 12th- Grade Educational Aspirations and Actual Education by Towns

Town	N	Av. SES	College	2–3 Yrs.	1 Year	HS
				Educational Aspirations*		
A	13	5.1	2 (3)	0 (1)	5 (4)	6 (5)
B-1	12	4.6	8 (3)	1 (0)	0 (4)	3 (5)
B-2	12	5.5	7 (1)	1 (0)	4 (8)	0 (3)
C	14	2.7	13 (11)	0 (0)	0 (0)	1 (3)
D-1	12	4.1	4 (2)	0 (1)	4 (5)	4 (4)
D-2	23	3.5	13 (11)	3 (1)	3 (5)	4 (6)
E	24	3.2	16 (13)	2 (1)	2 (7)	4 (3)

Town	N	Av. SES	College	2–3 Yrs.	1 Year	HS
				Actual Education		
A	13	5.1	0	1	2	10
B-1	12	4.6	1	0	3	8
B-2	12	5.5	0	2	8	2
C	14	2.7	6	5	1	2
D-1	12	4.1	0	0	6	6
D-2	23	3.5	4	6	6	7
E	24	3.2	4	8	9	3

*Grade 8 outside brackets; grade 12 inside brackets.

tions seem especially remarkable because we would consider grade 12 to be a clear cut-off point for decisions about college attendance. That is, if one has not made definite plans by that time, it would seem unlikely that college could be considered a realistic possibility. However, apparently the time served in the military service provides some kind of buffer zone in which one can re-analyze one's plans before absolute commitment to a job. In addition to this, of course, is the very important financial aid to education offered to veterans of the armed forces. It will be interesting to follow up young veterans and later compare their progress with other young men who did not have the experience of military life and veterans' benefits.

Our comparisons in this section of educational aspirations and the several variables have raised some interesting and, at times, disturbing trends. Our sample is limited in size and we do not intend to urge any definitive generalizations. We hope rather that we have suggested problems that can be further investigated with larger and more representative samples. Our data suggest that intelligence, social class, place of residence, and military service, have joint effects on educational aspirations and attainment. It was disturbing to find how often our brighter students from less affluent families or towns failed to follow through on their educational aspirations of early years, but encouraging to note that military service may lead to aspirations for higher attainment with some of our young people.

Vocational Maturity at Grade Twelve[3]

Although most analyses in this chapter are based on our HS + 4 years data, we include a study of the vocational maturity of our subjects at grade 12, using a set of behavioral characteristics not previously treated in depth in our research. This exploratory stage in career development is extremely important because it is at this point, career psychologists theorize, that the individual is crystalizing his vocational preferences and is about to commit himself to specific educational-occupational decisions that will vitally affect his future.

Vocational behavior characteristics of the exploratory stage can be categorized as search, experimentation, investigation, and trial. Their locus has been termed "self in situation" (Tiedeman and O'Hara 1963) and their essential purpose is to test the validity of some hypothesis or expectation about the self of the environment. Such behaviors include: searching for an appropriate outlet for one's interests and values, experimenting with adult vocational roles, seeking opportunities to demonstrate abilities, trying out new activities, orienting oneself to new situations, and striving for independence. (Super et al. 1963). When these activities are undertaken with the hope of eliciting information about oneself or one's environment, they become a means to increased self-knowledge and increased ability to relate this knowledge to future objectives.

Vocational maturity of the exploring adolescent should also be evidenced in his basic attitudes and perceptions. Satisfaction with a choice, confidence in plans, and enthusiasm over future prospects together with a congenial vocational self-concept are signs that the individual is dealing with vocational tasks successfully.

A favorable outcome of the process of exploration and hypothesis-testing should result in a realistic, integrated self-concept and clear formulation of objectives. The individual should be able to relate his/her special abilities, interests, and values to an occupational goal, clearly understanding why these personal attributes are at the basis of sound decisions. Formulation and implementation of specific plans for attaining this objective can then be carried out successfully.

In order to understand emergence of the vocational self-concept and assess career development, it is necessary to arrive at an operational definition for vocational maturity. This can be accomplished by a multivariable approach similar to that described by Super (1963). Vocational maturity is conceived in terms of coping behaviors and attitudes that are instrumental in the formation of an integrated

3. Catherine Lee is co-author of this section.

vocational identity and appropriate career objectives. These have been termed the dimensions of vocational maturity. For the purposes of this study, five dimension variables were selected because their contribution was felt to be essential to career development during the exploration years. They reflect the importance of an integrated value system, a sense of agency, and a feeling of high morale and self-esteem as attitudes and beliefs that are central to a vocational self-concept. The significance of role playing experiences and an understanding of the importance of informative advice were also explored as part of the process of career development.

Values

At the basis of every career decision, there is a hierarchy of personal values that organizes judgments, attitudes, and perceptions within the individual's self-concept, and musters them for decision making. Values may be considered as culturally influenced expressions of needs and the motivated reasons for which interests and goals are sought.

The source of an individual's value system is frequently the home. Family expectations, attitudes, and roles, as well a socioeconomic status influence the child's ideals and aspirations. Peer groups, especially during adolescence, are a major force in determining valued goals. However, since values are intimately related to inner psychological and physiological drives, their primary determinant is the person himself. Ginzberg (Ginzberg et al. 1951) has classified values as they relate to occupational preferences into three types: (1) related to the work activity itself; (2) related to the returns of work, as exemplified by pay and the way of life a job permits; or (3) related to the concomitants of work, what is associated with the job, such as coworkers and supervisors. The individual must be able to relate "work" values to an appropriate career goal. Capacities and interests must also be considered, but it is the value scheme that mediates an effective choice.

In crystallizing and implementing a career, the individual must relate his value hierarchy to the realities of environmental limitations. This process requires compromise among competing values and between values and opportunities. The value system is temporarily thrown out of balance, and change is necessitated. This alteration of values to eliminate contradictions between hopes and expectations is a necessary part of maturation and must occur before an individual can choose effectively.

Vocational maturity is evidenced in realistic appraisal of the personal value scheme in relation to future objectives. This study has sought to probe the student's awareness of values and their importance in career decision making. Information about valued activities and ideals must be understood as factors in occupational choice. If the individual knows what satisfaction he wants out of life and work, he is better able to set his course for a goal that will satisfy those values. Katz defines the value system as "the synthesizing element that orders, arranges and unifies such interactions, that ties together an individual's perceptions of cultural promptings, motivating needs, mediating symbols, differentiating characteristics, and sense of resolution that relates perceptions to self-concepts and that accounts most directly for a particular decision or for a mode of choosing." (Katz 1963, p. 16) It would seem that effective occupational choice is impossible without the support of values.

Sense of Agency

In addition to understanding the factors on which decision making should be based, the individual must possess a functioning belief that he *can* choose. This "awareness that he is an active agent in determining the course of his own career" is termed "sense of agency" (Tiedeman 1978). Sense of agency can be an attitude and an action. It is revealed first of all in self-esteem; the person must be confident of his or her abilities and be able to realistically set goals and limits. This confidence in self is basic to operating as an agent: "The individual must above all like himself . . .or his potential for manifesting agency behavior will remain latent." (Pincus 1968, p. 3) Self-direction and personal independence are also part of agency. The individual should display self-reliance, active involvement in directing his career, and satisfaction in making his own judgments. Finally, the self-directed individual is "committed"; he accepts responsibility for making a decision and seeing his plans through.

Agency is displayed by the individual who is satisfied with the choices he has made in the past and who is busy formulating specific plans to reach his occupational goal. He accepts "his assets and his liabilities in a realistic way, a way that does not hinder his performance" and realizes "his worth as an individual and is ready to capitalize on it." (Pincus 1968, p. 4) The student's readiness and ability to engage in career choice and to evaluate, modify, and achieve goals based on this choice is a basic criterion of career development.

Role Playing

"The complex self concept is organized within the framework of a role." (Super 1963, p. 18) One of the major vocational tasks of the adolescent is to explore the roles he may be expected to play and the opportunities to play roles that suit his personality, interests, and abilities. Role playing is carried on with the purpose of gaining information about the validity of some self-concept; it is what Jordan calls "hypothesis-testing."

Role playing begins with identification. The child who identifies with some significant adult strives in various ways to be like him. Eventually such identification becomes differentiated into occupational roles that can be tried out in fantasy and play. During adolescence, role playing comes to have greater significance. The student who aspires to be a research scientist takes part in science fairs and laboratory classes with this role in mind. Whether these roles are played in imagination, discussion, or are actually participated in, they give some opportunity to try on the role for size.

Role playing becomes reality testing when it is pursued in the "hope of eliciting information about oneself or one's environment, or of verifying or arriving at a basis for a decision." (Super et al. 1963, pp. 57-8) It is a trial in which the individual tests his performance in a role and discovers how well it agrees with his values and aptitudes. This also leads to greater understanding of the opportunities and expectation of various occupational roles and familiarizes the individual with alternatives that are open to him.

Students evidence occupational role playing by participating in school classes, clubs, part-time jobs, thoughtful discussion about careers, and even daydreaming. The ability to relate experiences in roles to one's abilities, values, and goals is an indication of vocational maturity.

Morale

Compromise between preferences and expectations is an essential part of the process of occupational choice. If the individual is able realistically to appraise his interests, abilities, values, strengths, and weaknesses and is also able to relate this knowledge of self to future objectives, the confrontation between self-concept and reality should be facilitated and prove satisfying. However, the individual who has not learned to deal with the developmental tasks of his career and has not achieved an integrated realistic self-concept will be unprepared to face limitations imposed by the environment. Poor planning, overestimation or underestimation of abilities, and lack of information about opportunities leave the individual with the single alternative of drifting into a potentially unsuccessful career. The result of all this will, of course, be disappointment, frustration, and depression, which will soon be reflected in all other aspects of the person's life. While low morale might be the result of overwhelming circumstances, this is the exception to the rule. Morale, thus, is an indicator of the past success, the present progress, and the future prospects of an individual's career.

Vocational maladjustment, like other emotional disturbances, is a symptom of the inability to cope with the problems of reality. Feelings of inevitability, uncertainty, and lack of enthusiasm are certainly not to be considered typical vocational attitudes in people who are about to face the challenges of the working world. The vocationally mature person is the one who expresses satisfaction with his career and with his total picture of himself.

Key Person

"Central in decisions about occupations, jobs, or courses of study are facts about one's self and about work." (Tiedeman 1978, p. 2) The individual is expected to use these facts to generate relevant information about those goals and alternatives that are most compatible with the self-concept. "The quality of decisions is ordinarily directly related to the quality and comprehensiveness of the information possessed by the decision maker. Even the most purposeful person is limited in a decision by the lack of complete information." (Tiedeman 1967, p. 11)

The aware student realizes that, although the execution of a vocational decision is his responsibility, informed and experienced adults can help him to realize his full potentiality. Guidance counselors in the school are not only able to provide facts relevant to courses, training, and occupations but they are also able to aid the student in translating these data into relevant information. In addition, people working in preferred occupations, students in a relevant training program, and other informed adults can provide valuable insights.

The student who does not take advantage of the aid these people can offer and who has not yet learned the role of information in vocational decisions has no means of coping with developmental tasks. Accurate and comprehensive information about alternatives and consequences obtained from reliable sources and informed adults is a key to career success.

Vocational Maturity Scoring Criteria

To develop the vocational maturity scoring criteria, 106 12th-grade protocols (4 interviews were eliminated for various reasons) were read in their entirety and questions were selected that were felt to measure each of the following 5 12th-grade vocational maturity scales (VM12):

1. Values
2. Sense of Agency
3. Role Playing
4. Morale
5. Key Person

The 12th-grade interview schedule is reproduced in the Appendix of Gribbons and Lohnes, 1969.

Eight interviews, selected at random, were used in preparing the scoring manual. Responses from these protocols were studied, criteria for assigning scores were defined, and representative verbatim answers were selected to illustrate the quality of information expected for each scale. The main criteria for scaling were quality of response, accuracy of information, and awareness of an indicated dimension of vocational maturity. Emphasis was not on the occupation chosen, but on the reasons for the choice and the student's ability to relate his self-appraisal to an appropriate goal. Responses indicative of average vocational maturity were scored 1 and were expected to reveal understandings of the process of vocational decision making and integration of vocational information and choice. A score of 2 was given for responses that indicated superior maturity, highly adequate vocational coping behavior, and a well-developed decision process. Below average responses received a score of 0; they revealed little understanding of the importance of vocational choice or of the factors on which it is based.

Ten questions supplied background material. They supplied general information concerning each student's high school curriculum, special test scores, educational plans, occupational goals, activities, and scholastic ability.

The scorer had a good understanding of the process of career development and was thoroughly familiar with the interview and the scoring manual. Only one VM12 dimension was scored at a time for each student protocol.

Reliability of Scales

A formal reliability study was not undertaken because the generalizations behind the scales are very tentative and would not seem to justify the time and expense such a study would require. In an informal check of intrajudge reliability, however, the scorer rerated all interviews one week after the original scoring on two variables— Values and Sense of Agency—which had often presented scoring problems. About 90% of the scores agreed across trials and those that did not differ by only one point.

Results

The mean scores (table 2.11) for the 106 subjects indicate that the males earn slightly higher scores than do the females—6.5 vs. 5.9. Twenty-two males but only 11 females score in the 8 to 10 point range, also indicating a slight edge on the part of the males to score higher on this 12th-grade measure of vocational maturity.

When the individual scale scores are examined, it is quite clear that most of the scores, for both sexes, fall into the 1 to 2 point range, with Morale coming closest to a normal distribution of scores. It is also apparent that, with the exception of Sense of Agency, the males' average scores are slightly higher on the individual 12th-grade vocational maturity scales.

Table 2.11. Distribution of VM12 Scores

		Distribution for Total Sample	
		Males	Females
Score	N	N 54	N 52
0–5	36	16	20
6–7	37	16	21
8–10	33	22	11
Mean	6.2	6.5	5.9
S.D.	2.38	2.02	2.63

		Distribution by Sex for 5 VM12 Scales							
			Sense of		Role				Key
VM Score	Values		Agency		Playing		Morale		Person
	M	F	M	F	M	F	M	F	M	F
0	3	6	7	5	4	7	9	7	8	7
1	31	27	25	26	26	23	29	38	17	22
2	20	19	22	21	24	22	16	7	29	23

Table 2.12. Distribution of VM12: Educational, Occupational, and
Socioeconomic Class Variables

		VM12 SCORES		
Variable	**N**	**0–5**	**6–7**	**8–10**
Intelligence				
111 plus	42	13	11	17
100–110	45	14	21	10
99 below	20	9	5	6
Socioeconomic				
Status Level				
1–2	24	5	10	9
3–5	60	21	19	20
6–7	22	10	8	4
Curriculum				
College Prep.	55	14	20	21
Business	34	15	12	7
IA-General	17	7	5	5
Educational				
Aspirations				
College	45	10	16	19
Post High School	32	13	11	8
High School	29	13	10	6
Roe Levels				
2–3	64	12	26	26
4–7	42	24	11	7

Although examination of table 2.12 might suggest some slight relationship between IQ and VM scores, the evidence is far from clear. For
example, 17 of 42 of the 111-Plus IQ students score in the high VM12
range, but 13 of the same group fall at the lowest end of the scale. The
overall results do not appear to indicate a strong relationship between
VM and IQ.

There does appear to be a relationship between SES (rating of
father's occupation according to Hamburger scale) and VM12. Almost
twice as many (12 + 5) subjects at high SES levels earned high VM
scores, the reverse tendency is noted for low SES levels, and the
middle SES subjects are spread quite evenly throughout the range of
the 10 point scale.

Twelfth-grade curriculum enrollment seems to be related to VM
scores; more college preparatory students earn high VM scores, while
Business and 1A-General students generally earn lower scores.

Examination of the 12th-grade educational aspiration data indicates that far more college aspirants score in the high range (19) than in
the low range (10), and subjects with no educational aspirations beyond

the 12th grade show a complete reversal of this pattern (6 high vs. 13 low).

Roe's levels of occupational aspirations were combined into two groups, and it is quite clear that subjects who show a preference for higher level occupations also score higher on the 12th-grade measure of vocational maturity.

The instrument designed to measure 12th-grade vocational maturity has demonstrated some interesting trends. Males, subjects in higher SES levels, college curriculum students, those aspiring to education beyond high school, and those aspiring to higher levels of occupations all score higher on this measure of vocational maturity. There appears to be no strong relationship between IQ and vocational maturity.

Because these results are based on an instrument whose reliability has not been established, they must be considered as very tentative.

The authors feel, however, that they do suggest that 12th-graders, on the average, are coping adequately with their vocational tasks, have come to understand the important factors in their decision making, and realize, at least tacitly, the need to integrate the self-concept into the process of career choice. If one's self-concept conveys a picture of satisfaction and success in an occupational role, the individual is likely to initiate activities that will advance his goal and brings its implementation closer. The relationships that have been noted between vocational maturity and curriculum, social status, and vocational aspirations can be understood as part of this relationship. Seeing oneself as the product of an economically and socially successful home, as an educated and respected member of the professions, is certainly more likely to stimulate career implementation than the expectations of a laborer's son who envisions his future as an inevitable repetition of his father's unhappy drudgery. This situation has important implications for counseling. Positive attitudes, self-understanding, and a well-developed vocational repertoire are the means to vocational success; without them, all the ability and opportunity in the world are lost.

Seventeen is a fascinating age from which to view an emerging career for it is the time when the individual begins to sight his approaching goal and can feel his power over the future course of his career. He waits on the brink of so many important insights into his self-concept and into the process of implementing a vocational choice. In Super's words, this is the time when

> . . . young people explore the world in which they live, the subculture of which they are about to become a part, the roles they may be expected to play, and the opportunities to play roles which suit

their personalities, interests, and aptitudes. It is at the same period in which the adolescent through experience and self-examination clarifies his self-concept and begins to put it into words, finds out what outlets exist in society for one who seeks to play a given role, and modifies his self-concept to bring it in line with reality. Adolescent exploration is, in this view, a process of attempting to develop and implement a realistic self-concept. (Super 1963, p. 25)

Relating Vocational Maturity in Early Adolescence to Nine-Year Career Patterns Criteria

In their 1957 framework for research on career development, Super and his associates elucidated a construct they called *vocational maturity*. This construct has dominated the psychology of career development in the 20 years since the publication of that crucial theoretical framework. The key word in Super's original exposition of the construct is "evaluation." The trait indicators of vocational maturity in adolescence require evaluation by the psychologist for the extent to which, in his judgment, they presage achievement of the goal of integrative vocational adjustment in adulthood. There is a "criterion of long-term efficiency in attaining satisfaction of socialized goals" (Super et al. 1957, p. 70) which is the standard for rating adolescent behaviors for their degree of vocational maturity. A recent extensive review of Super's Career Pattern Study has characterized that longitudinal research program as follows:

> Perhaps most important is the exposition of a dependent, or criterion, set of variables as the class of dimensions of integrative vocational adjustment. The basic research paradigm which emerges is to scale the independent variables as dimensions of vocational maturity by relating them to the dimensions of the criterion. (Cooley and Lohnes 1968, pp. 4–15)

In short, the main justification of vocational maturity traits is to be their power as predictors of subsequent career adjustments. Published longitudinal research results have demonstrated weak but positive predictive powers for VM scales in the Career Pattern Study data (Super et al. 1967) and in the data of the parallel Career Development Study (Gribbons and Lohnes 1968). Here we extend the results of the latter study to data collected 4 years after the 111 male and female subjects graduated from high school, or 9 years after the initial interviews in the 8th grade.

The initial 8th-grade data of the Career Development Study were collected by interviewing in 1958. The 9-year follow-up data were collected by interviewing and inventorying in 1967. All analyses referred to here as previously reported can be found in *Emerging Careers* (Gribbons and Lohnes 1968). In the 8th-grade data, vocational maturity was treated as a syndrome of 8 moderately correlated traits, called, as a set, Readiness for Vocational Planning (RVP). The 8 1958 RVP scale scores of the subjects are related to several career patterns criteria in this report. However, a continuing research problem for the CDS has been the artificial overdetermination of the subjects by the predictors, especially since this has prevented the teaming of other interesting predictor variables, such as intelligence, with the vocational maturity scales. There simply are not enough degrees of freedom made available by 111 subjects to convincingly relate 8-plus predictor scales to criteria, particularly if the criterion variable is a taxonomy in several categories. Classification criteria have had to be forced into dichotomies, frequently with real loss of meaning. Therefore, a major objective of this report is to explore the possibility of recovering degrees of freedom by substituting a univariate treatment of vocational maturity for the RVP syndrome. The new univariate scaling is called *Readiness for Career Planning* (RCP). The 22 items selected by factor analysis procedures from the original 45 items of the 8th-grade interview and scored for RCP are listed in table 2.13. It is hoped that the retreat to a single scale for a subset of the 1958 VM indicators will be justified by the opportunities it creates to team a VM measure with other predictors and to employ more detailed taxonomic criteria.

The additional predictors from early adolescence to be incorporated with RCP are sex, socioeconomic status, and intelligence. Table 2.14 contains the intercorrelations among these variables, and their means and standard deviations, for the 8th-grade data. The strongest relationship among the 4 variables is a moderate tendency for intelligence to increase with increasing socioeconomic status of family. RCP is not significantly correlated with sex or socioeconomic status, and its correlation with intelligence is modest. This .31 correlation can be compared with the previously reported multiple correlation of the 8 RVP scales with intelligence of .57, which suggests that the RCP scale is freer of contamination with intelligence than are the RVP scales as a set. These 4 relatively independent predictors seem to represent a suitably parsimonious yet potentially powerful antecedent measurement space for a longitudinal study with the modest sample size of the CDS.

The criterion scaling problem has been a bugaboo that the CPS and CDS have attempted to reduce through a series of approximations of assorted worthiness. It is one thing to speak philosophically of the

Table 2.13. Eighth-grade Interview Items Scored for Readiness for
Career Planning (RCP)

1. What curricula are there that you can take in the 9th grade?
2. Why did you decide to take _____ curriculum?
3. Why did you decide not to choose one of the other curriculums?
4. Why did you decide not to choose a second of the other curriculums?
5. Is there any advantage to taking the college curriculum?
6. Are these advantages in taking the other curriculums?
7. What facts should you know about yourself before you choose a curriculum?
8. How can you predict your chances of success in different courses for next year?
9. Is there any advantage to taking algebra?
10. Why would you like to become a __(first choice)__?
11. What facts should you know about yourself before choosing an occupation?
12. How much education is required to be a __(first choice)__?
13. What does a __(first choice)__ do at work?
14. What connections do you see between the subjects you'll be taking next year and the work you want to do later on?
15. Which abilities do you have that will help you to be successful in your program for next year?
16. Which ability do you lack that you feel would help you to be successful in your high school program?
17. Which abilities do you have that will help you in the work you are planning?
18. Which ability do you lack that you feel would help you to be successful as a __(first choice)__?
19. What particular interests and activities would your occupation satisfy?
20. As you know, things that are important to us are called values. Tell me some of your values.
21. What values of yours would working as a __(first choice)__ satisfy?
22. Suppose your parents didn't agree with your plans. What would you do?

goal of integrative vocational adjustment; it is another to choose operational indicators of progress toward this panacea. Similarly, it is easier
to talk about career patterns than to decide how to quantify them for
research manipulations. In order to evaluate a trend in a subject's
vocational adjustment it is necessary to look simultaneously at data
from at least 2 points in his life history, so that what is evaluated is a

Table 2.14. Intercorrelations, Means, and Standard Deviations for Four 8th-grade
(1958) Variables
(N = 110)

		SES		Mean	S.D.
Sex (male = 1; female = 2)	.01	.03	− .18	1.5	.6
Socioeconomic Status (1 = hi; 7 = lo)		− .35	− .14	4.0	1.6
Otis Beta Form Intelligence			.31	107.9	9.5
Readiness for Career Planning				32.4	10.8

transition from time 1 to time 2. Super (1963) has defined a set of 5 *coping behaviors* that seem to represent the best available rubric for evaluating transitions in career development data. These coping behavior categories are: (1) floundering, (2) trial, (3) stagnation, (4) instrumentation, and (5) establishment. Since the CDS subjects have been interviewed 5 times at 2-year intervals, it has been possible to score 4 transitions for coping behaviors, using the categories as an exclusive and exhaustive taxonomy. Unfortunately, 5 unequally populated cells are about 2 or 3 too many for multivariate statistical analysis of data on 111 subjects. It was necessary to pool the coping behaviors of floundering and stagnation into a single category, which might then be called "unsatisfactory adjustment transitions," and to pool the other 3 coping behaviors into what might be called "satisfactory transitions," particularly to permit multivariate analysis of variance (MANOVA) in the measurement space of the 8 RVP variables. The present strategy is to report parallel studies of criteria in the 2 spaces of (1) the 8 RVP scales, and (2) the 4 predictors of table 2.14, in order to compare results.

When the 1958/61 transitions were judged, 70 subjects were rated as "unsatisfactory" and only 40 were rated as "satisfactory." These are fairly global clinical ratings that take into account both the occupational and educational aspirations in both years and the actual educational or occupational placements. That there is some lawfulness apparent in the ratings over 4 transitions is evidenced by previously reported fitting of Markov chain theory to the data. Looking at the separation of the 2 groups of 1958/61 ratings in the space of the 8 1958 RVP scales, as shown in table 2.15, it appears that the RVP syndrome does not significantly separate the groups. Only Evidence for Self-Ratings displays a marked contrast between the groups, and that in a contratheory direction. Turning to table 2.16, it can be seen that there is also a failure of separation of the criterion groups in the space of the 4 predictors. The "satisfactory" group has better RCP, intelligence, and socioeconomic status (and more females), but the trend is not significant.

In the light of this failure of short-range predictive validity for the two predictor sets, it is not surprising that the transitional coping behavior groups for the most remote transition, 1965/67, are not significantly separated in either of the measurement spaces. Table 2.17 shows that, of the 8 RVP scales, Evidence for Self-Ratings provides the only significant contrast between the groups. The "satisfactory" group is about one-half a standard deviation higher on this variable than is the "unsatisfactory" group. Evidence for Self-Ratings is based

Table 2.15. MANOVA Study
(Criterion is 1958/61 transitional coping behavior ratings; group 1 (N = 70)
floundering or stagnation; group 2 (N = 40) trial, instrumentation, or establishment;
predictors are 1958 eight RVP scores)

RVP Variables	Group 1 Means	Group 2 Means	Group 1 S.D.'s	Group 2 S.D.'s	F^1 108
Factors in Curriculum Choice	15.4	15.6	6.5	5.9	.0
Factors in Occupational Choice	14.3	15.2	4.7	4.5	.9
Verbalized Strengths and Weaknesses	6.1	6.9	3.0	3.7	1.5
Accuracy of Self-Appraisal	7.1	7.0	1.5	1.3	.3
Evidence for Self Ratings	1.6	1.2	1.2	1.2	4.2
Interests	4.2	3.9	2.1	2.4	.8
Values	3.1	3.2	2.6	2.4	.0
Independence of Choice	4.4	4.3	1.9	1.8	.1

NOTE: For equality of dispersions, MANOVA $F_\infty^{36} = 1.2$; for equality of centroids, MANOVA $F_{101}^8 = 1.2$.

on judgments of the quality of the evidence cited by the subject in defense of his appraisal of his own abilities. It should be noted that the interview protocol items that combine to form this scale in the RVP system are not items that enter into scoring RCP. Table 2.18 reveals that for the 1965/67 transition the "satisfactory" group again has better RCP, intelligence, and socioeconomic status, but again to insignificant

Table 2.16. MANOVA Study
(Criterion is 1958/61 transitional coping behavior ratings; group 1 (N = 70)
floundering or stagnation; group 2 (N = 40) trial, instrumentation, or establishment;
predictors are 1958 sex, SES, IQ, RCP

Predictors from Eighth grade (1958)	Group 1 Means	Group 2 Means	Group 1 S.D.'s	Group 2 S.D.'s	F^1 108
Sex (male = 1; female = 2)	1.5	1.6	.6	.5	1.7
Socioeconomic Status (1 = hi; 7 = lo)	4.0	3.9	1.6	1.7	.0
Otis Beta Form Intelligence	107.7	108.4	9.1	10.2	.1
Readiness for Career Planning	31.7	33.7	10.7	11.0	.9

NOTE: For equality of dispersions, MANOVA $F_\infty^{10} = 1.0$; for equality of centroids, MANOVA $F_{105}^4 = .8$.

Table 2.17. MANOVA Study
(Criterion is 1965/67 transitional coping behavior ratings; group 1 (N = 51)
floundering or stagnation; group 2 (N = 58) trial, instrumentation or establishment;
predictors are 1958 eight RVP scores)

RVP Variables	Group 1 Means	Group 2 Means	Group 1 S.D.'s	Group 2 S.D.'s	F^1 107
Factors in Curriculum Choice	14.8	15.8	6.3	6.2	.8
Factors in Occupational Choice	14.4	14.6	4.7	4.8	.0
Verbalized Strengths and Weaknesses	6.2	6.6	3.5	3.1	.4
Accuracy of Self-Appraisal	6.9	7.1	1.4	1.4	.8
Evidence for Self-Ratings	1.1	1.7	1.2	1.2	7.4
Interests	4.0	4.1	2.5	1.9	.0
Values	3.0	3.2	2.5	2.7	.3
Independence of Choice	4.2	4.5	1.9	1.8	.8

NOTE: For equality of dispersions, MANOVA F^{36}_∞ = .8; for equality of centroids, MANOVA F^8_{100} = 1.0.

extents. It is interesting that, in the latest ratings, a majority of 58 subjects has been judged "satisfactory" and a minority of 51 has been judged "unsatisfactory." Perhaps this shift in the populations of the 2 categories from the 1958/61 transition in early adolescence to the 1965/67 transition in early adulthood represents a real gain in the per-

Table 2.18. MANOVA Study
(Criterion is 1965/67 transitional coping behavior ratings; group 1 (N = 51)
floundering or stagnation; group 2 (N = 58) trial, instrumentation, or establishment;
predictors are 1958 sex, SES, IQ, RCP)

Predictors from Eighth grade (1958)	Group 1 Means	Group 2 Means	Group 1 S.D.'s	Group 2 S.D.'s	F^1 107
Sex (male = 1; female = 2)	1.5	1.5	.6	.5	.0
Socioeconomic Status (1 = hi; 7 = lo)	4.2	3.8	1.6	1.7	1.8
Otis Beta Form Intelligence	107.1	108.5	9.1	9.9	.6
Readiness for Career Planning	31.3	33.2	10.8	10.7	.9

NOTE: For equality of dispersions, MANOVA F^{10}_∞ = .5; for equality of centroids, MANOVA F^4_{104} = .6.

centage of subjects who are making reasonable progress toward their goals, and not just a softening of the standards of judgment. We hope so.

The fact that the subjects responded to a number of inventories in the 1967 data collection provides an opportunity to view the predictability of the latest coping behavior ratings from the measurement base of 11 inventory scales in a concurrent validity study. The first inventory scale, *Occupational Aspirations,* is adapted from Haller and Miller's instrument of the same name. High scores indicate personal preferences for high status occupations. The *Work Beliefs* scale is also adapted from Haller and Miller's inventory of the same name. High scores indicate beliefs about such matters as mobility, scheduling, and promptness that are judged to be conducive to success in the world of work. The 4 interest scales, *Business, Outdoors* and *Shop, Cultural,* and *Science,* are adaptations of the Project TALENT interest inventory, and the remaining 5 scales, *Conformity, Impulsion, Sociability, Leadership,* and *Introspection,* are adaptations of the Project TALENT temperament survey. The 9 scales based on Project TALENT items follow quite closely the outcomes of Lohnes' (1966) factor analysis of the motives domain in the Project TALENT battery. However, all these item pools were created for and tested on youth of high school age, and their use with young adults 4 years out of high school is experimental, to say the least.

Table 2.19 contains the concurrent validity study results. Only one of the inventory scales separates the groups by an amount approaching one-half of a standard deviation, and that is Conformity, on which the group rated "unsatisfactory" scores higher. In the Lohnes theory, the Conformity variable represents an unintelligent global response set much like Edwards' social desirability factor, making this a convincing contrast between these two groups of young adults. Table 2.19 also shows the "unsatisfactory" group to be at a disadvantage with respect to Occupational Aspirations, Business Interest, Cultural Interest, and Science Interest. It is not surprising that they should be higher on Outdoors and Shop Interests or on Sociability, but their slight edge on Work Beliefs and larger edge on Introspection are contratheory. In general, the concurrent validity of this 11-scale inventory battery appears to be real but weak.

The 11 inventory scales are part of a set of 22 variables we have scaled from the 1967 protocols. The other variables include a masculinity-femininity scale based on the Project TALENT Interest items, 4 scales based on the positions of the 1967 occupational aspirations and the 1967 occupational placement in the Anne Roe occupational group

Table 2.19. MANOVA Study
(Criterion is 1965/67 transitional coping behvior ratings; group 1 (N = 48) floundering
or stagnation; group 2 (N = 58) trial, instrumentation, or establishment; predictors
are 11 1967 inventory correlates)

1967 Self-report Inventory Scales	Group 1 Means	Group 2 Means	Group 1 S.D.'s	Group 2 S.D.'s	F^1 104
Occupational Aspirations	40.8	42.0	9.3	11.2	.4
Work Beliefs	32.5	32.1	3.8	3.6	.3
Business Interest	81.2	89.5	30.7	33.1	1.8
Outdoors Shop Interest	83.0	79.4	41.9	38.4	.2
Cultural Interest	88.4	92.2	27.7	25.2	.5
Science Interest	43.3	45.5	20.3	31.5	.3
Conformity	46.5	41.7	10.5	12.2	4.6
Impulsion	2.8	2.7	1.9	1.9	.0
Sociability	8.2	7.5	2.7	2.8	1.8
Leadership	1.6	1.5	1.4	1.6	.1
Introspection	80.	7.0	2.7	2.9	2.9

NOTE: For equality of dispersions, MANOVA F_x^{66} = 1.1; for equality of centroids,
MANOVA F_{94}^{11} = 1.2.

and occupational level structures, and 6 additional clinical-type ratings
of aspects of the protocols. These "22 correlates" can be thought of as
a set of criterion scales to which to relate the 1958 predictor sets by
correlation procedures. Tables 2.20, 2.21, and 2.22 provide details on a
rank 7 canonical correlation model relating the 8 1958 RVP scales to
these 22 correlates from 1967. Once again, there is no strong, robust

Table 2.20. Canonical Correlation of 1958 Eight RVP Scales with 1967 Twenty-Two
Correlates (N = 105); Rank 7 Model

Factor Set	Canonical R	1958 Eight RVP		1967 Twenty-two Correlates	
		Percent Variance	Percent Redundancy	Percent Variance	Percent Redundancy
1	.67	15.3	6.9	8.6	3.9
2	.53	14.1	4.0	4.4	1.2
3	.51	13.0	3.4	5.7	1.5
4	.46	11.8	2.4	7.1	1.5
5	.44	9.9	2.0	2.9	.6
6	.38	17.0	2.4	4.9	.7
7	.37	9.6	1.3	4.8	.7

NOTE: Totals for rank 7 model: Variance extracted from 1958 8-RVP = 90.7%; redundancy of 1958 8-RVP = 22.4%; variance extracted from 1967 22-scales = 38.4%;
redundancy of 1967 22-scales = 10.1%.

Table 2.21. Canonical Correlation Factors of 1958 Eight RVP Scales

	Canonical Factors						
RVP Variables	**1**	**2**	**3**	**4**	**5**	**6**	**7**
Factors in Curriculum Choice	.67		.57			.29	− .33
Factors in Occupational Choice			.41		.59		
Verbalized Strengths and Weaknesses	.55				.53		.44
Accuracy of Self-Appraisal		.70	.34			− .42	− .27
Evidence for Self-Ratings	.44	.52		− .67			
Interests	.37	.42		.60		.27	
Values	.27		.59		− .29	.33	.57
Independence of Choice		.29				.87	

NOTE: Entries are factor-scale correlations, with coefficients smaller than .25 edited out for clarity.

Table 2.22. Canonical Correlation Factors of 1967 Twenty-Two Correlates

	Canonical Factors						
Twenty-two Scales	**1**	**2**	**3**	**4**	**5**	**6**	**7**
Occupational Aspirations	.52						
Work Beliefs			.25	.36			.47
Business Interest		.27	− .26	.63	.29		
Outdoors Shop Interest		.40		.45			
Cultural Interest			.39				.42
Science Interest				.41		− .26	
Masculinity-Femininity	− .26	.43		.39			
Conformity	− .37		− .43		.25		.26
Impulsion					− .25		
Sociability							.26
Leadership				.37		.50	
Introspection					.35	.29	
Actual Roe Group	.44		.29				
Roe Group Aspirations	.35						
Actual Roe Level	− .38	.33	− .30				
Roe Level Aspirations	− .46						
Realism	.32						
Commitment	.59						
Parental Relations						.62	
Plans Certainty			.35	− .40		.29	
Adjustment		− .29	.45		.36		
DCP Rating			− .30				.29

NOTE: Entries are factor-scale correlations, with coefficients smaller than .25 edited out for clarity.

finding. Even this high-rank model accounts for little of the variance in the 22 correlates (38%) and displays little ostensible redundancy of the 1958 battery, given the total variance of the 1967 battery (22%), and even less redundancy of the 1967 battery, given the total variance of the 1958 battery (10%). Neither of the canonical factor patterns displays any approach to simple structure.

The canonical correlation relation of the 1967 22 correlates with the 4 1958 predictors are presented in Tables 2.23 and 2.24. These relations are stronger than those with the 8 1958 RVP scales, but this is because there is a definite sex effect for a number of the 22 correlates and sex is one of the 4 predictors. The first canonical factor for each sex displays this sex linkage. The magnitudes of the second and third canonical correlation coefficients in this study (.64 and .52) are very close to those of the first and second in the preceding study (.67 and .53). For both the second and third canonical relations, socioeconomic status loads higher on the prediction function than either intelligence or RCP.

The transitional coping behaviors data had one strike against them to start with, namely, their basic subjectivity as evaluations placed on protocols of subjects by the researcher. The results just reported add the second strike of weak predictability from the antecedent variables of interest in this inquiry. Nevertheless, we will keep these data in the game for the two reasons that they represent the best approximation we can muster to scaling Super's very convincing construct of coping behaviors, and that they do succeed in displaying an innate orderliness in our Markov chain analyses of them. We may yet discover more meaningful relations of these data with other variables in the life histories of our subjects as we know them. Meanwhile we have to look for other career adjustment scales against which to try to demonstrate more convincingly the predictive potency of our vocational maturity measures.

The Career Development Tree

The CDS has in the past relied heavily on Anne Roe's (Roe and Siegleman 1964) constructs of occupational levels and occupational groups as criterion scales, placing the occupational aspirations of the subjects at the different developmental stages in these two taxonomic variables. The 8th-grade RVP syndrome has been shown to be a valid predictor of Roe level of occupational aspiration at every one of the four developmental stages previously reported, and of Roe group of

Table 2.23. Canonical Correlation of 1958 Four Predictors with 1967 Twenty-Two Correlates (N = 105)
Rank 3 Model, with Canonical Factors of 1958 Data)

Factor Set	Canonical R	1958 Four X		1967 Twenty-Two X	
		Percent Variance	Percent Redundancy	Percent Variance	Percent Redundancy
1	.84	28.0	20.0	9.6	6.8
2	.64	33.7	13.6	14.4	5.8
3	.52	19.7	5.3	2.7	.1

NOTE: Totals for rank 3 model—variance extracted from 1958 predictors = 81.4%; redundancy of 1958 predictors = 38.9%; variance extracted from 1967 22-scales = 26.7%; redundancy of 1967 22-scales = 12.7%.

	Canonical Factors		
1958 Variables	1	2	3
Sex	.97	− .33	− .11
Socioeconomic Status	.22	.70	.62
Otis Intelligence	− .07	− .32	− .56
Readiness for Career Planning	.08	.56	− .54

Table 2.24. Canonical Correlation Factors of 1967 Twenty-Two Correlates

	Canonical Factors		
Twenty-two Scales	1	2	3
Occupational Aspirations	.36	− .47	
Work Beliefs			
Business Interest	.38	.33	
Outdoors Shop Interest	.27	.51	
Cultural Interest			
Science Interest	.38		
Masculinity-Femininity		.42	
Conformity			.31
Impulsion			.26
Sociability			
Leadership	.43		
Introspection	.35		
Actual Roe Group	.42	− .38	
Roe Group Aspiration	.64		
Actual Roe Level	− .34	.62	
Roe Level Aspiration	− .66	.29	
Realism		− .65	.25
Commitment		− .69	
Parental Relationships		− .42	
Plans Certainty		− .42	− .39
Adjustment		− .28	
DCP Rating		.41	

NOTE: Entries are factor-scale correlations, with coefficients less than .25 edited out for clarity occupational aspirations at the most remote stage previously reported. That is, 8th-grade RVP yielded significant prediction of Roe group of aspiration 2 years out of high school. Successful Markov chain fittings have also been previously reported for these 2 Roe criterion variables. One of the problems with the Roe variables is that they are anything but independent, and are in theory the 2 axes of a lattice system containing 48 cells. No research program to date has been able to employ the lattice system successfully as a criterion variable. It has too many cells to serve as a factorial analysis of variance design, especially since the correlation of the factors of the design leads inevitably to practically empty cells in some regions. It cannot be worked as a 2-element vector variable because the scale positions on the group axis are strictly nominal. The problems with the Roe lattice are compounded when one tries to use it repeatedly in longitudinal studies such as the CPS or the CDS, where a rather small sample of subjects is observed many times, because the resulting 3-dimensional lattice really has a plethora of cells. Roe's group and level constructs are essential aspects of the theory of career development, but some refinements of scaling beyond the Roe lattice appear to be necessary.

Cooley and Lohnes (1968) have capitalized on the extensive longitudinal data files of Project TALENT to refine a sequential structure of occupational taxonomy variables, inspired jointly by Roe's constructs and the construct of developmental stages as proposed by Ginzberg et al. (1951) and improved by Super et al. (1957). One of the major virtues of the Career Tree Structure arranged by Cooley and Lohnes is that its categories for occupational aspirations at each age level have been selected to be highly discriminable in suitable personality measurement spaces, as indicated by extensive computing on the Project TALENT data. Another attractive feature of the model is that the level of complexity of the taxonomic variable increases over time as a function of increasing vocational maturity, yet each new level of complexity is achieved by application of a simple dichotomous choice rule. Figure 2.1, reproduced from Cooley and Lohnes (1968, p. 4–57), represents the tree structure model.

The earliest dichotomization or branching in the tree is premised on Anne Roe's people-thing continuum (Roe and Siegelman 1964). In Figure 2.1 the numbers in boldface under each branch node report the part of a nominal 1,000 males that the Project TALENT estimates, based on tens of thousands of males in a national probability sample, place at that node. Thus it is estimated that of 1,000 boys entering junior high school about 560 would be classed as primarily "thing" oriented and about 440 as primarily "people" oriented. The next

Figure 2.1 Project TALENT Career Development Tree (Cooley and Lohnes 1968)

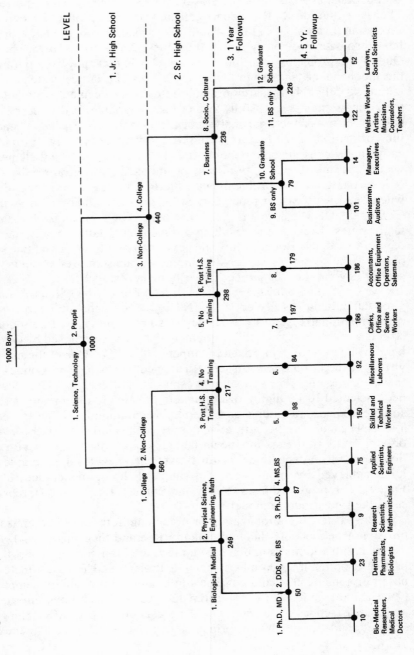

Figure 2.2 Career Development Study Tree

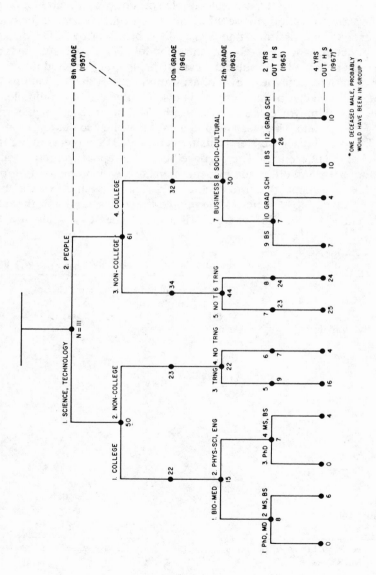

dichotomization is based on whether or not the subject is planning to attend a 4-year college, and so on. Eventually the 12-branch tips of the tree provide a 12-category taxonomy of occupations or occupational aspirations for young adults, which is as complex as the view of the world of work promoted by this model ever gets. Even so, it is apparent that studies with the modest sample sizes of the CPS and CDS will not be able to use all the detail of the 12-category variable for many purposes. Figure 2.2 distributes the 111 subjects of the CDS through the branchings of the tree structure model. Note that substantially fewer than half of the subjects persist in aspiring to graduate from college, and the 2 highest level of aspiration cells at the branch tips are empty of subjects in this sample. The sole subject who would clearly have persevered to cell 3, Ph.D. in physical science or engineering, was a young man who was killed in an automobile accident.

Chapter 4 discusses the transitions of the CDS subjects in the tree model at greater length. The purpose here is to report predictive validity studies for the 8th-grade measurement sets which employ criterion variables based on the tree. Table 2.25 reports a study of the 1958 career tree variable, which is the people-thing dichotomy, in the measurement space of the 1958 8 RVP scores. The RVP scales do not

Table 2.25. MANOVA Study
(Criterion: 1958 Career Tree Variable; Predictors 1958 Eight RVP Scores; N = 110)

	Orientation Groups		Pooled Groups	
	Sci-Tech	People		
	(N = 49)	(N = 61)	est.	F^1
1958 RVP Variables	Means	Means	S.D.'s	108
Factors in Curriculum Choice	16.5	14.7	6.2	2.3
Factors in Occupational Choice	14.2	14.9	4.6	.6
Verbalized Strengths and Weaknesses	6.3	6.6	3.3	.2
Accuracy of Self-Appraisal	7.0	7.1	1.4	.1
Evidence for Self-Ratings	1.5	1.4	1.2	.3
Interests	4.2	4.1	2.2	.1
Values	3.0	3.2	2.6	.1
Independence of Choice	4.5	4.3	1.9	.2

NOTE: For equality of dispersions, MANOVA $F_\infty^{36} = 1.3$; for equality of centroids, MANOVA $F_\infty^8 = .9$.

Table 2.26. MANOVA Study
(Criterion: 1958 Career Tree Variable; Predictors: 1958 Sex, SES, IQ, and RCP;
N = 110)

Predictors from Eighth-grade (1958)	Orientation Groups		Pooled Groups	
	Sci-Tech (N = 49) Means	People (N = 61) Means	Est. S.D.'s	F^1 108
Sex (male = 1; female = 2)	1.2	1.7	.5	29.4
Socioeconomic Status (1 = high; 7 = low)	3.6	4.3	1.6	5.0
Otis Beta Form Intelligence	107.8	108.0	9.6	.0
Readiness for Career Planning	33.4	31.7	10.8	.6

NOTE: For equality of dispersions, MANOVA $F_x^{10} = 1.1$; for equality of centroids, MANOVA $F_{105}^4 = 9.4$.

provide a basis for predicting the concurrent tree variable. Table 2.26 reports the parallel study in the space of the 4 1958 predictors. Here there is dramatic separation of the 2 criterion groups, but neither intelligence nor RCP contributes to the contrast. Sex is the big separator, with a preponderance of boys displaying a science and technology orientation and a majority of girls showing a humanistic, sociocultural orientation. There is also a significant socioeconomic status contrast, with the science and technology oriented youths enjoying higher status as a group than do the humanistic, sociocultural oriented youths. It is theoretically satisfactory that the vocational maturity measures should not have concurrent validity for this basic interests orientation in early adolescence, because if they did have it would simply indicate an interests contamination in the maturity measures, which would be no more acceptable than a substantial intelligence contamination would be.

The 1961 10th-grade tree criterion has four cells, reflecting both basic interests and whether the subject plans to attend college. As shown in table 2.27, the 8 RVP scales do provide a basis for significant prediction of this variable. Factors in Curriculum Choice provide the strongest predictor, with the effects indicating that the 2 college planning groups have given more careful thought to curriculum selection than the 2 noncollege groups. Table 2.28 shows that the contrasts among the criterion groups are very strong in the space of the 4 predictors. Sex continues to be the strongest predictor, but there is a good, strong relationship between RCP and the criterion. The comparison of the modest predictive validity of intelligence with the strong validity of RCP is noteworthy.

The next six tables (tables 2.29–2.34) report predictive validity studies for the 1963, 1965, and 1967 career tree variables. Several

Table 2.27. MANOVA Study
(Criterion: 1961 Career Tree Variable; Predictors: 1958 eight RVP scores; N = 110)

RVP	College Science (N = 22) Means	Orientation Groups Noncoll Technol. (N = 22) Means	Noncoll Business (N = 34) Means	College Bus-Cult (N = 32) Means	Pooled Groups Est. S.D.'s	F^3 106
I	16.7	15.4	12.6	17.8	6.0	4.5
II	13.9	13.9	14.2	16.1	4.6	1.6
III	7.2	6.1	5.2	7.4	3.2	3.1
IV	7.4	6.6	7.1	7.1	1.4	1.2
V	1.9	1.3	1.2	1.6	1.2	1.8
VI	5.1	3.3	3.6	4.5	2.1	3.6
VII	3.0	3.1	2.3	4.0	2.5	2.6
VIII	4.3	4.3	3.9	4.9	1.8	1.4

NOTE: For equality of dispersions, MANOVA $F_x^{108} = 1.2$; for equality of centroids, MANOVA $F_{287}^{24} = 1.6$.

trends are apparent. The predictive validity of the 1958 8 RVP scales increases steadily over time! This can be seen by comparing the centroids MANOVA F-ratios for 1961 = 1.6 (table 2.27); 1963 = 1.7 (table 2.29); 1965 = 2.0 (table 2.31), and 1967 = 2.3 (table 2.33). There is an irregular trend for the predictive validity of the 1958 4 predictors to increase over time. The centroids F-ratios are 1961 = 4.6 (table 2.28); 1965 = 2.0 (table 2.30); 1965 = 6.6 (table 2.32); and 1967 = 6.3 (table 2.34). All four predictors are potent at every followup year, but sex and RCP are the stronger predictors in 1961 and 1963, whereas socioeconomic status moves to first place in 1965, and both SES and intelligence are stronger than sex and RCP in 1967. We are, of course, especially pleased with the robust univariate F-ratios for RCP for all four followup years. These are:

Table 2.28. MANOVA Study
(Criterion: 1961 Career Tree Variable; Predictors: 1958 Sex, SES, IQ, and RCP; N = 110)

Four Scales	College Science (N = 22) Means	Noncoll Technol. (N = 22) Means	Noncoll Business (N = 34) Means	College Bus-Cult (N = 32) Means	Pooled Groups Est. S.D.'s	F^3 106
Sex	1.2	1.3	1.9	1.5	.5	8.7
SES	3.5	4.1	4.6	3.4	1.6	3.9
IQ	110.0	104.6	106.6	110.3	9.4	2.2
RCP	33.9	31.6	27.0	37.8	10.1	6.5

NOTE: For equality of dispersions, MANOVA $F^{30} = 1.8$; for equality of centroids, MANOVA $F_{272}^{12} = 4.6$.

Career Tree	RCP
Year	*F-ratio*
1961	6.5
1963	6.1
1965	7.6
1967	4.6

In the career tree data for 9 years, almost one-half of the subjects display patterns of transitions in their aspirations that can be classified as "path-following." Each of the path-followers traces one of the 12 branches provided in the career tree. The majority of the subjects can be classified as "path-jumping," since at least once they make a transition in aspiration that removes them from one of the 12 branches and transports them to some other branch. (To more nearly balance the populations in the two groups, the authors have classified as path-followers 8 subjects who followed noncollege branches strictly over the 4 transitions observed but who, in the most recent 1965/67 transition, jumped from either no post-high school training to some post-high school training, or the other way. This is viewed as a modestly meaningful jump in comparison to the other available jumps.) For people who are path-followers, expressed aspiration at any time is, of course, the best prediction of what the aspiration will be at a later time. For path-jumpers, Cooley and Lohnes argue that a probability law governing their migrations can be phrased:

> Our research and that of others shows that migration from one stable career path to another (or path-jumping) tends to take the individual to a path for which he is closer to the centroid. That is,

Table 2.29. MANOVA Study
(Criterion: 1963 Career Tree Variable; Predictors: 1958 Eight RVP Scores; N = 110)

RVP	College Science (N = 15) Means	Noncoll Technol. (N = 21) Means	Noncoll Business (N = 44) Means	College Bus-Cult (N = 30) Means	Pooled Groups Est. S.D.'s	F^3 106
I	17.2	14.8	13.3	17.9	6.0	4.0
II	13.9	13.6	13.9	16.4	4.7	2.4
III	6.9	6.1	5.3	8.0	3.1	4.7
IV	7.3	6.6	7.1	7.1	1.4	.8
V	2.2	1.1	1.2	1.8	1.2	4.9
VI	4.1	3.5	3.8	5.1	2.2	3.0
VII	2.7	2.7	2.6	4.3	2.5	3.3
VIII	4.2	4.0	4.3	4.8	1.9	.9

NOTE: For equality of dispersions, MANOVA $F_{\times}^{108} = .9$; for equality of centroids, MANOVA $F_{287}^{24} = 1.7$.

Table 2.30. MANOVA Study
(Criterion: 1963 Career Tree Variable; Predictors: 1958 Sex, SES, IQ, and RCP; N = 110)

Four Scales	College Science (N = 15) Means	Noncoll Technol. (N = 21) Means	Noncoll Business (N = 44) Means	College Bus-Cult (N = 30) Means	Pooled Groups Est. S.D.'s	F^3 106
Sex	1.1	1.4	1.8	1.4	.5	6.4
SES	3.5	4.1	4.5	3.3	1.6	3.8
IQ	112.5	103.5	106.3	111.0	9.1	4.6
RCP	33.5	29.9	29.0	38.7	10.1	6.1

NOTE: For equality of dispersions, MANOVA F_{∞}^{30} = 1.5; for equality of centroids, MANOVA F_{272}^{12} = 4.4

Table 2.31. MANOVA Study
(Criterion: 1965 Career Tree Variable; Predictors: 1958 Eight RVP Scores; N = 110)

RVP	College Science (N = 15) Means	Noncoll Technol. (N = 15) Means	Noncoll Business (N = 47) Means	College Bus-Cult (N = 33) Means	Pooled Groups Est. S.D.'s	F^3 106
I	19.0	12.1	13.5	17.9	5.7	7.6
II	14.6	12.4	14.2	15.9	4.7	2.0
III	7.3	5.6	5.7	7.5	3.2	2.8
IV	7.9	6.2	7.0	7.0	1.4	4.1
V	1.9	1.2	1.2	1.8	1.2	3.1
VI	4.4	4.0	3.5	4.8	2.2	2.4
VII	3.8	1.7	2.7	4.0	2.5	4.1
VIII	4.7	4.1	4.4	4.3	1.9	.3

NOTE: For equality of dispersions, MANOVA F_{∞}^{108} = 1.3; for equality of centroids, MANOVA F_{287}^{24} = 2.0.

Table 2.32. MANOVA Study
(Criterion: 1965 Career Tree Variable; Predictors: 1958 Sex, SES, IQ, and RCP; N = 110)

Four Scales	College Science (N = 15) Means	Noncoll Technol. (N = 15) Means	Noncoll Business (N = 47) Means	College Bus-Cult (N = 33) Means	Pooled Groups Est. S.D.'s	F^3 106
Sex	1.3	1.1	1.8	1.4	.5	8.3
SES	3.3	4.5	4.7	3.0	1.5	10.5
IQ	111.6	103.1	105.8	111.5	9.0	4.9
RCP	37.0	26.7	29.1	37.7	9.9	7.6

NOTE: For equality of dispersions, MANOVA F_{∞}^{30} = .8; for equality of centroids, MANOVA F_{272}^{12} = 6.6.

Table 2.33. MANOVA Study
(Criterion: 1967 Career Tree Variable; Predictors: 1958 Eight RVP Scores; N = 109)

RVP	College Science (N = 10) Means	Noncoll Technol. (N = 19) Means	Noncoll Business (N = 49) Means	College Bus-Cult (N = 31) Means	Pooled Groups Est. S.D.'s	F^3 105
I	17.4	13.2	13.7	18.5	5.9	5.5
II	12.7	12.9	14.3	16.3	4.6	2.8
III	5.8	6.0	5.7	7.9	3.2	3.4
IV	8.0	6.5	7.0	7.0	1.4	2.5
V	2.0	1.1	1.1	2.0	1.2	5.4
VI	3.1	3.6	3.9	5.0	2.1	3.1
VII	3.0	2.7	2.6	4.2	2.5	3.1
VIII	4.5	4.8	4.3	4.1	1.9	.7

NOTE: For equality of dispersions, MANOVA $F_\times^{108}$ = 1.2; for equality of centroids, MANOVA F_{284}^{24} = 2.3.

changing plans so that his career pattern is classified as unstable usually decreases the generalized distance of the individual from his group's centroid in a suitable personality measurement space. This change law is perhaps the most significant finding of psychometric research on career variables. (Cooley and Lohnes 1968, p. 5–4).

An interesting issue is the possible predictability of who will be a path-jumper and who will be a path-follower. Sex is a predictor, since more females are path-followers than are males. Table 2.35 indicates that 8th-grade RVP measures are a basis for predicting this dichotomy, with jumpers scoring higher than followers on the two best predictors, which are Factors in Curriculum Choice and Accuracy of Self-

Table 2.34. MANOVA Study
(Criterion: 1967 Career Tree Variable; Predictors: 1958 Sex, SES, IQ, and RCP; N = 109)

Four Scales	College Science (N = 10) Means	Noncoll Technol. (N = 19) Means	Noncoll Business (N = 49) Means	College Bus-Cult (N = 31) Means	Pooled Groups Est. S.D.'s	F^3 105
Sex	1.3	1.3	1.8	1.4	.5	6.6
SES	3.7	4.4	4.6	2.8	1.5	9.8
IQ	113.1	101.1	106.3	112.8	8.6	9.2
RCP	32.8	30.2	29.4	37.9	10.2	4.6

NOTE: For equality of dispersions, MANOVA $F_\times^{30}$ = 1.2; for equality of centroids, MANOVA F_{270}^{12} = 6.3.

Table 2.35. MANOVA Study
(Criterion: 1958–67 Career Tree Structure Behaviors; Predictors: 1958 Eight RVP Scores; N = 110)

1958 RVP Variables	Path-Followers (N = 51) Means	Path-Jumpers (N = 59) Means	Pooled Groups Est. S.D.'s	F^1 108
Factors in Curriculum Choice	13.9	16.6	6.1	5.1
Factors in Occupational Choice	15.0	14.1	4.7	1.1
Verbalized Strengths and Weaknesses	6.7	6.2	3.3	.6
Accuracy of Self Appraisal	6.8	7.2	1.4	2.0
Evidence for Self Ratings	1.6	1.4	1.2	.7
Interests	4.3	3.9	2.2	.9
Values	3.0	3.2	2.6	.1
Independence of Choice	4.2	4.5	1.9	.9

NOTE: For equality of dispersions, MANOVA $F_z^{36} = 1.0$; for equality of centroids, MANOVA $F_{101}^8 = 2.3$.

Appraisal. Table 2.36 displays the sex contrast and indicates that RCP is a significant predictor of this criterion behavior, with the path-jumpers scoring higher on this vocational maturity scale than do the path-followers. There would seem to be an important implication for

Table 2.36. MANOVA Study
(Criterion: 1958–67 Career Tree Structure Behaviors; Predictors: 1958 Sex, SES, IQ, and RCP, N = 110)

Predictors from Eighth grade (1958)	Path-Followers (N = 51) Means	Path-Jumpers (N = 59) Means	Pooled Groups Est. S.D.'s	F^1 108
Sex (male = 1; female = 2)	1.6	1.4	.6	4.5
Socioeconomic Status (1 = high; 7 = low)	4.2	3.8	1.6	1.5
Otis Beta Form Intelligence	108.3	107.6	9.6	.1
Readiness for Career Planning	30.7	34.0	10.7	2.6

NOTE: For equality of dispersions, MANOVA $F_z^{10} = 1.9$; for equality of centroids, MANOVA $F_{105}^4 = 2.1$.

Table 2.37. MANOVA Study
(Criterion: 1958–67 Career Tree Structure Behaviors; Predictors: Eleven 1967
Inventory Scales; N = 106)

1967 Self-report Inventory Scales	Path-Followers (N = 48) Means	Path-Jumpers (N = 58) Means	Pooled Groups Est. S.D.'s	F^1 104
Occupational Aspirations	38.4	44.0	10.0	8.5
Work Beliefs	32.4	32.3	3.7	.0
Business Interests	82.3	88.6	32.1	1.0
Outdoors Shop Interests	78.6	83.1	40.0	.3
Science Interests	90.2	90.7	26.4	.0
Cultural Interests	39.0	40.9	20.3	6.5
Impulsion	2.6	2.9	1.9	1.0
Sociability	7.6	8.1	2.8	.8
Leadership	1.4	1.6	1.5	.2
Introspection	6.8	8.0	2.8	5.4
Conformity	45.7	42.3	11.6	2.3

NOTE: For equality of dispersions, MANOVA $F_x^{66} = 1.1$; for equality of centroids, MANOVA $F_{94}^{11} = 2.0$.

career development theory in this finding that people whose occupational aspirations over the span from early adolescence to early adulthood follow a simple tree structure model tend to be rated as less vocationally mature in early adolescence than those whose patterns violate the simple structural model. The data of table 2.37 reinforce this implication by showing that on inventory scales in early adulthood (1967) the path-jumpers have higher occupational aspirations, stronger cultural interests, more introspection, and less conformity than the path-followers. Note in table 2.36 that the jumpers are not more intelligent and enjoy only a slight advantage in socioeconomic status of family, yet the suggestion is that in some ways the jumpers who break the rules of the tree structure are stronger people.

Summary and Conclusions

Published predictive validities of vocational maturity scales collected in early adolescence can be characterized as weak but positive. To some extent the research problem has been to find more appropriate follow-up criteria for vocational maturity scales. This section has reported predictive validity studies for two sets of variables collected on 110 subjects when they were in the eighth grade. The first set is eight Readiness for Vocational Planning (RVP) scales. The second set is sex, socioeconomic status, Otis intelligence, and Readiness for Career Planning (RCP), which is a unitary vocational maturity scale from a subset of the RVP items. Both RVP and RCP are relatively free of correlation with sex, socioeconomic status, and intelligence.

A series of studies involving transitional coping behaviors as the criteria once again showed only disappointing degrees of predictive validity for RVP and RCP. Canonical relations of both sets of predictors with a set of 22 1967 correlates were relatively weak, except for sex linkages.

The breakthrough occurred when a set of criteria were scaled from a career tree structure model for transitions in educational and occupational aspirations over time. RVP and RCP were both robustly related to the career tree variables at all points in time, with a regular trend for RVP validity to increase over time. Comparative validities of sex, socioeconomic status, and intelligence were reported.

Path-following versus path-jumping in the career tree is moderately predictable, and there are indications that the pathjumpers as a group are the stronger people.

3
Trial: Six Years Beyond High School

CDS conducted a sixth data collection in early 1969, when the average age of the subjects was almost 25. According to Super's developmental model (table 1.1), they were probably completing the last, or Trial, substage of Exploration, in which final vocational commitments were likely to crystallize. Two young men were dead, one in an automobile accident and the other in the Vietnam War. One young man who completed college could not be located. As shown by table 3.1, slightly more than half the subjects were currently married, with more women married than single. (There had been half a dozen divorces, and three of the currently single women were divorcees.)

Table 3.1. Marital Status of CDS Subjects in 1969

Sex	Married	Single	Total
Male	26	28	54
Female	30	24	54
Total	56	52	108

Two problems, one per sex, have plagued us in our analyses of career patterns; they have also plagued many subjects in their career adjustments. For the men, the problem is their military obligation, which we can only view as a disaster for personal and scientific rationalization of career development. For the women, the problem is the construction to be placed personally and scientifically on housewifery. Fortunately the latter problem seems to disturb the analysts more than it does the women. It is noteworthy that 44% of the young women were still single six years beyond high school. For them at least the rubrics of career development were indisputably relevant. For the rest, we can only join them in their oft-stated conviction that housewifery is

Table 3.2. Sex X Career Tree Branch Tips Frequencies

	Career Tree Branch Tips				
Sex	CS	NT	NB	CB	Total
Male	4	18	19	13	54
Female	5	4	40	5	54
Total	9	22	59	18	108

a proud vocation and, by itself or intermixed with other occupations, the basis for a meaningful career.

Throughout this report we have relied heavily on a four-category criterion variable inspired by the Career Development Tree (Cooley and Lohnes 1968). This variable combines the basic orientation dichotomy of technology orientations ("thing") versus sociocultural and business orientations ("people") with the basic educational level dichotomy of college versus noncollege. Thus we have these groups:

Mnemonic	Career Tree Group
CS	College Science
NT	Noncollege Technology
NB	Noncollege Sociocultural and Business
CB	College Sociocultural and Business

Although the full tree model has 12 branch tips (see Figures 2.2 and 2.3), we have employed only these 4 major branches because of

Table 3.3. Sex X Orientation

	Orientation		
Sex	Things	People	Total
Male	22	32	54
Female	9	45	54
Total	31	77	108

our small sample size. We will argue later that this 4-fold discrimination is a nonetheless a sufficiently detailed mapping of the world of work for junior high school guidance purposes. Table 3.2 reports the

Table 3.4. Sex X Education

	Education		
Sex	College	Noncollege	Total
Male	17	37	54
Female	10	44	54
Total	27	81	108

Table 3.5. 1958 and 1969 Sample Proportions in Tree Groups

	Career Tree Branch Tips			
Year	CS	NT	NB	CB
1958	.30	.15	.22	.33
1969	.08	.20	.55	.17

frequencies for the 4 categories by sex and for the total sample, while table 3.3 displays the basic orientation breakdown by sex, and table 3.4 the college versus noncollege sex breakdown. Only 25% of our subjects had achieved, or were still pursuing, a college education in 1969, as contrasted with 53% whose 8th-grade self-concepts included expectations of a college education. That 17 males and only 10 females have arrived in the college category 6 years beyond high school is foreshadowed by the 8th-grade break of 38 boys and 20 girls expecting to achieve college degrees. That the majority of males falls into the "thing" orientation category and the majority of females into the "people" orientation category is not surprising. That only 28% of all our subjects have arrived in science or technology vocations does tend to temper our appraisal of this as a technological civilization.

The Markov chain data tables reported in tables 4.1 and 4.2 show the history of this career tree variable in our investigation through the 1967 data. It is interesting to compare the proportions of subjects whose 8th-grade aspirations placed them in each of the 4 categories in 1958 with the proportions for 1969, as presented in table 3.5. The remarkable growth of membership in the NB category is due mainly to the fact that few girls identified housewifery as a career goal in 1958, while many have chosen or accepted it as such in 1969. Table 3.6 brings the chain transitions data up to 1969. This final observation distribution is *not* reasonably close to the theory matrix fitted to the first 3 transitions (table 4.2), but it is not entirely unlike it either. The diagonal values are rather similar. This late in the game, however, there are a number of off-diagonal transitions that are not being made by any or

Table 3.6. Final Transition Proportions for Career Tree Variable for 1967–69 (Frequencies in Brackets)

1967 Groups	1969 Career Tree Groups							
	CS		NT		NB		CB	
CS	.46	(5)	.18	(2)	.09	(1)	.27	(3)
NT	.05	(1)	.68	(13)	.26	(5)	.00	(0)
NB	.00	(0)	.06	(3)	.94	(46)	.00	(0)
CB	.10	(3)	.17	(5)	.23	(7)	.50	(15)

Table 3.7. Markov Chain Theory Matrix Fitted to Five Observed Transitions between 1958 and 1969

	Career Tree Branches			
	CS	NT	NB	CB
CS	.53	.21	.03	.23
NT	.13	.65	.13	.09
NB	.01	.05	.91	.03
CB	.04	.07	.23	.66

NOTE: For stationarity hypothesis, $\chi_{48}^2 = 67$, $p < .01$; for order one versus order two, $\chi_{36}^2 = 62$, $p < .01$; for order zero versus order one, $\chi_9^2 = 618$, $p < .001$.

many of the subjects. Table 3.7 shows a Markov chain theory matrix fitted to all 5 available transition matrices. Comparison with table 4.2 indicates it to be remarkably like the theory matrix fitted to the first 3 transitions, but the increased numbers of degrees of freedom for the 2 goodness of fit tests that we want not to reject now lead to rejections on both (whereas we had previously accepted stationarity and rejected order oneness). Our overall impression is that the behavior of our subjects over 11 years on this career goals variable is too complex to be described adequately by a simple probability model. This conclusion reassures us that we have in hand a suitable criterion variable for attempts at trait-statistical prediction.

Predicting Terminal Career Goals from 8th-Grade Traits

Are the 1969 career tree branch memberships of the CDS men and women contingent on their 1958 values for the personality factors of intelligence (IQ) and vocational maturity (RCP)? Are these terminal goals contingent on the 1958 socioeconomic status (SES) of their families? How contingent on sex is the career tree variable in this final observation of it? What is the best linear combination of these four predictors for this terminal view of the criterion? How has the predictability of the career tree categories changed over time? The multivariate analysis of variance (MANOVA) and multiple group discriminant analysis provide a data analysis strategy for inferences on these questions. Table 3.8 reports the required MANOVA study. It ranks the contingency relations in this order: SES, IQ, and sex, with RCP a poor fourth. Review of Table 2.34 indicates that, for the career tree criterion measured in 1967, the MANOVA ranking of the predictors was the same, although the fourth-place F value for RCP was not as weak. Review of tables 2.28 and 2.30 reminds us that in the high school years of 1961 (10th grade) and 1963 the rankings were different, with sex and RCP showing the strongest predictive validities for the career tree branches. Perhaps the most interesting feature of table 3.8 is that the highest RCP mean does *not* belong to the group that has the best SES and IQ means.

The multivariate eta-square value of .41 for the 1969 tree criterion in the space of the 4 predictors reveals only a modest shared variance between criterion and predictors. However, the values of .48 and .49 for this statistic when the criterion was measured in 1967 and 1958 (table 3.9) indicate that the strength of the overall contingency, never very strong, does not fall off radically over the 11 years. These values are comparable to canonical correlation coefficients in the .65 to .70 range and are not negligible. Table 3.9 enables us to compare the best linear discriminant functions for the tree criterion in the space of the 4 1958 predictors when the criterion is measured in 1958, 1967 and 1969. The best functions (df1) for 1967 and 1969 are very much alike, correlating strongly with SES and IQ, and the second best functions (df2) for these years are also similar, although the emphasis switches from IQ and sex in 1967 to sex and IQ in 1969. In the 1967 and 1969 studies, df1 separates the two college groups from the two noncollege groups, and df2 tends to separate the predominantly male noncollege technology group from the other 3 groups. However, in the 1958 study it is df2 *based on RCP* that separates the college from the noncollege groups, while df1 based on sex separates the 2 "thing" oriented groups from the 2 "people" oriented groups. The details of the 3 discriminant analyses differ sufficiently to reinforce our conviction that the dynamics of this

Table 3.8. MANOVA Study
(Criterion: 1969 Career Tree Variable; Predictors: 1958 Sex, SES, IQ, and RCP; $N = 108$)

	Career Tree Groups					
	College Science	Noncoll Technol.	Noncoll Business	College Bus-Cult	Pooled Groups	
Four	($N = 9$)	($N = 22$)	($N = 59$)	($N = 18$)	Est.	F^3
Scales	Means	Means	Means	Means	S.D.'s	104
Sex*	1.6	1.2	1.7	1.3	.5	6.8
SES†	2.2	4.3	4.4	3.0	1.5	8.9
IQ	115.6	103.2	106.6	113.6	8.7	7.4
RCP	33.3	32.6	30.9	37.8	9.1	2.0

NOTE: For equality of dispersions, MANOVA $F_x^{30} = .7$; for equality of centroids, MANOVA $F_{267}^{12} = 5.0$, $\eta^2 = .41$.
*Male = 1; female = 2.
†Highest socioeconomic status = 1; lowest status = 7.

Table 3.9. Correlations of Two Discriminant Functions with the Four 1958 Predictors for Discrimination of Career Tree Criterion Groups in 1958, 1967, and 1969 data (Eta [canonical R] and Proportion of Predictor Battery Extracted by Each Discriminant, and Criterion Group Centroids on Discriminant Functions*

Predictors	1958		1967		1969	
	df1	df2	df1	df2	df1	df2
Sex	− .87	.02	− .47	.68	− .37	.87
SES	− .43	− .43	− .75	− .08	− .82	− .17
IQ	− .04	.50	.59	.73	.67	.49
RCP	.06	.92	.54	.08	.37	− .16
Eta (canon R)	.56	.50	.61	.38	.54	.40
Variance Extracted	.24	.32	.35	.25	.35	.26
Group Centroids						
College Science	.40	.45	.50	.18	1.03	.50
Noncoll Technol.	.92	− .81	− .23	− .80	− .12	− .73
Noncoll Business	− .72	− .52	− .54	.23	− .37	.23
College Sociocultural and Business	− .29	.28	.85	.06	.84	− .10
MANOVA eta-square	.49		.48		.42	

Functions have unit standard deviation for total samples

career goals variable, viewed as a process variable over 11 years of crucial development, are complex and changing. That the changes are in the direction of increased dependence on adolescent SES and IQ is sobering, especially as we ponder the well-known interdependence, premised partly on genetic mechanisms, of these 2 predictors. We have to feel that our subjects are working out their fates as well as their plans in what Super has aptly termed the "process of compromise."

Table 3.10 reports classifications of the subjects into predicted 1969 tree groups computed from their 1958 trait profiles, sorted according to their actual 1969 group memberships. A majority of the CS, NT, and NB groups are correctly classified, but only 38% of the actual CB group members are placed in the CB group. Why some of these college sociocultural and business subjects, who "look more like" college science subjects, are not pursuing science or technology careers is a nice question.

Since the level of educational attainment is particularly valued in our society, we have looked at it in greater detail in a MANOVA study reported in table 3.11. Again we see that SES is the strongest indicator, with IQ also a strong indicator. The really remarkable thing about table 3.11 is that, with but one slight discrepancy (RCP means for the graduate school and BS or BA groups), the 5 groups are colinear on all 4 variables, and we may summarize the study with the generalization that educational attainment in early adulthood increases with increas-

Table 3.10. Classification Outcomes for 1969 Tree Groups in Space of 1958 Sex, SES, IQ, and RCP
(All Entries Are Percentages of Row Totals) (N = 108)

	Predicted Groups				
Actual Groups	CS	NT	NB	CB	Actual %
CS	66	0	22	11	8
NT	4	63	18	13	20
NB	13	27	52	6	54
CB	27	22	11	38	16
Predicted Percentage of total N	18	31	36	13	

NOTE: Total percentage of hits = 53; total percentage of misses = 47.

ing early adolescent SES, IQ, maleness, and RCP of subsamples. One discriminant function absorbs almost all the discriminating power of the battery, as we might expect from the colinearity of the groups, and the groups are properly aligned on it. The correlations of the predictors with df1 are: SEX $-.31$; SES $-.85$; IQ .72; RCP .27, and the canonical correlation of df1 with the weighted function of the group memberships is .62. The discriminant function extracts 35% of the predictor battery variance. Note that the MANOVA η^2 for this study is very similar to that for the 1969 career tree criterion.

Summary

We observe with sadness that our small group of young men has not escaped the scythes of the war in Vietnam and the war on our

Table 3.11. MANOVA Study
(Criterion: 1969 Educational Attainment in Five Levels; Predictors: 1958 Sex, SES, IQ, and RCP; N = 108)

	1969 Levels of Educational Attainment						
Four Scales	Grad. School (N = 10) Means	BS or BA (N = 12) Means	HS + 2 or 3 yrs (N = 21) Means	HS + 1 yr (N = 27) Means	HS only (N = 38) Means	Pooled Groups Est S.D.'s	F^4 103
Sex	1.3	1.3	1.4	1.5	1.6	.5	1.0
SES	2.0	3.3	3.5	4.0	4.9	1.4	10.6
IQ	118.3	112.3	109.6	105.2	104.5	8.6	6.8
RCP	35.1	37.3	33.6	31.3	30.8	10.8	1.1

NOTE: For equality of dispersions, MANOVA $F^{40} = .7$; for equality of centroids, MANOVA $F^{16}_{306} = 3.6$, $\eta^2 = .41$; for this criterion in space of 1958 eight RVP scales, MANOVA $F^{32}_{355} = 1.07$ and $\eta^2 = .29$.

highways. With some surprise we note that, at average age of almost 25, over half of the CDS men and almost half of the women are single, and that only one quarter of the subjects have achieved or are still pursuing a four-year college education. Similarly surprising is that only about one-quarter are placed terminally in science or technology vocations. In the 8th grade, fully half the subjects expected to achieve four-year college educations, and 45% planned on science or technology vocations. Particularly problematic is why the large majority of our college-achieving males has finally eschewed science or technology careers. Their military service obligations have perturbed the career patterns of the men in many ways. Housewifery has emerged as a chosen or accepted career for many women who did not nominate it when they were interviewed in the 8th grade.

The Markov chain theory fitted to the first three transitions on the Career Development Tree variable never did fit the data very well, but in the 1969 data, signs remain of some coherence between the theory and the data. A Markov chain fitted to all the available data for five transitions is remarkably similar to the one fitted to the first three transitions. The impression is that much of the variance in the career tree patterns needs to be explained by external predictors.

The trait-statistical prediction of the 1969 career tree tips distribution showed the strongest relations to 1958 SES and IQ, even as in the 1967 criterion data. This finding is in marked contrast to the finding of strongest contingencies with sex and 1958 RCP in the 1958, 1961, and 1963 criterion data. Our impression is that the career tree variable is a complex process variable the dynamics of which depend less on self-concepts and more on the hard realities of social status and intelligence as the subjects mature vocationally. Level of educational attainment as a terminal value for the educational aspiration process variable appears to be constrained by the same dynamics as the career tree variable tips, and the shifts over time are much the same for both processes. These studies of 11-year career patterns convince us that our subjects are integrating their fates and their plans through a dialectic of compromise.

4
Probability Models for Career Patterns

The trait model of measurement is easily employed to predict a criterion measure at time 2 from a predictor measure at time 1, even if both measures are multivariate. However, development surveys that employ a nominal adjustment criterion observed repeatedly over several, or many, time intervals pose a design problem that has not been adequately solved. What is the appropriate prediction model for relating antecedent trait measures to a posterior time series on a nominal variable? In such a case the criterion data follow a multivariate multinominal distribution, a form with which we have little experience. The initial attractiveness of the Markov chain stems from the simple fact that it provides an analysis of a time series on a nominal variable. The Markov chain is a powerful model for such data, in that it yields many insights and useful predictions for any development process that follows a probability law of the chain type. On the other hand, the power of the model is purchased at the price of a set of restrictive assumptions that few development processes are likely to satisfy. Our thesis is that the most interesting variability in a development process scaled as a time series on a nominal variable is the variability not accounted for by the best fitting Markov chian. The ability of a psychometric prediction system to improve on the predictions from the Markov chain may provide the most convincing demonstration of the predictive validity of the antecedent trait measures for the development criterion.

Lohnes (1965) reviewed the features of Markov chains that are useful for human development surveys, and Gribbons and Lohnes (1968) reported a series of Markov chain analyses of career development data in their book on the Career Development Study (CDS). Recently the availability of ten-year follow-up data from that longitudinal study has permitted the testing of predictions from the reported chains. Reflection on the implications of the successes and failures of

Table 4.1. Observed Transitions in Career Goals as Proportions of Row Totals (Frequencies in Brackets)

		1958 (Eighth-Grade Distribution		
CS	College Science		.30	(33)
NT	Noncollege Technology		.15	(17)
NB	Noncollege Business, Cultural		.22	(24)
CB	College Business, Cultural		.33	(37)

Transition 1 (1958–61)							
	CS		**NT**		**NB**		**CB**
CS	.49 (16)	.30 (10)	.03 (1)	.18 (6)
NT	.12 (2)	.59 (10)	.12 (2)	.17 (3)
NB	.04 (1)	.04 (1)	.79 (19)	.13 (3)
CB	.08 (3)	.06 (2)	.32 (12)	.54 (20)

Transition 2 (1961–63)							
	CS		**NT**		**NB**		**CB**
CS	.54 (12)	.23 (5)	.05 (1)	.18 (4)
NT	.13 (3)	.65 (15)	.09 (2)	.13 (3)
NB	.00 (0)	.06 (2)	.94 (32)	.00 (0)
CB	.00 (0)	.00 (0)	.28 (9)	.72 (23)

Transition 3 (1963–65)							
	CS		**NT**		**NB**		**CB**
CS	.60 (9)	.00 (0)	.00 (0)	.40 (6)
NT	.23 (5)	.64 (14)	.04 (1)	.09 (2)
NB	.02 (1)	.02 (1)	.89 (39)	.07 (3)
CB	.00 (0)	.04 (1)	.23 (7)	.73 (22)

those predictions led to the point of view submitted below by references to a new Markov chain analysis of CDS data.

The new Markov variable was inspired by the Project TALENT career tree structure (Cooley and Lohnes 1968, ch. 4). It is a 4-cell nominal variable that classifies occupational aspirations according to (1) whether they reflect primarily a thing orientation or a people orientation (following Roe and Siegelman 1964), and (2) whether or not they involve a college baccalaureate degree. Table 4.1 identifies the 4 groups and shows the original 8th-grade distribution of the 57 boys and 54 girls. The 10-year followup distribution of the 57 boys and 54 girls is figurable as the column sums of bracketed frequencies in the second part of table 4.2, i.e., Transition 4 (1965–67). Thus, while 33 subjects aspired to College Science (CS) careers in 8th grade, only 11 subjects aspire to such careers 10 years later; and while only 24 subjects were interested in Noncollege Business and Cultural careers in 8th grade, 49 subjects accept such careers as their lot as young adults. It would seem that many of the goals held in early adolescence turned out to be unrealistic. There is considerable development in aspirations over the 10-year period to be explained.

A Markov chain analysis begins with the tabulation of the actual transition frequencies for each observation interval and converts these to proportions of row totals. In each such table the rows represent the states of the variable at the earlier stage and the columns represent the states of the variable at the later stage. Thus, in table 4.1 (Transition 1 (1958–61), the rows report the Markov variable for 8th grade and the columns for 10th grade. Each number in brackets is the frequency of transitions from that row state in 1958 to that column state in 1961. For example, 16 subjects who expressed CS aspirations in 1958 expressed CS aspirations again in 1961. These 16 persevering subjects were .49 of all those who expressed CS aspirations in 1958. The other half migrated in 1961 to the other 3 cells in the frequencies and proportions shown, the biggest migrant group being the 10 subjects who retained their thing orientation but gave up their college plans. Notice that this first transition matrix is diagonally dominated, meaning that for every category the largest proportion of the 1958 entrants is made up of those who retained that aspiration in 1961. Transition 2 (1961–63) and Transition 3 (1963–65) also show strong diagonal domination. Notice that over the years there is very little recruitment into the CS and NT groups from the NB and CB groups. Those who are people-oriented in early adolescence retain that orientation for the most part into early adulthood.

Table 4.1 provides interesting data reduction but no theory. Markov chain theorizing assumes that there is a constant transition probabilities matrix for the population, from which each of the observed transition matrices deviates only due to sampling fluctuations. This assumption of constant probabilities for transitions that do not depend on the place in the time series of the transitions observed is a very strong assumption. Another assumption is that the process has one-step memory, in that the probabilities of the various outcomes for a subject at any transition are dependent only on his state of input to that transition, and not at all on his earlier history as reflected in the path by which he arrived at his input state. This is an almost ridiculous assumption to make about a human development process, but we point out that it is not nearly as ridiculous as the alternative hypothesis, that the transitions represent a random walk, or a process with no memory whatever. We suggest that the Markov chain provides a better null hypothesis for such data than the random walk that is usually invoked.

The best fitting Markov chain for the data is induced by a maximum likelihood method described by Anderson and Goodman (1957). The fitted constant transition matrix (also called the stationary, or theory, matrix) for our data is reported at the top of table 4.2. Notice that it appears to be a sort of an average of the three actual transition matrices. The chi-square tests that come next in Table 4.2 assure us

Table 4.2. Markov Chain Theory Matrix and Tests of Theory

| | **Stationary Transition Matrix** | | | |
	CS	**NT**	**NB**	**CB**
CS	.53	.21	.03	.23
NT	.16	.63	.08	.13
NB	.02	.04	.88	.06
CB	.03	.03	.28	.66

Stationarity Hypothesis $\chi 24^2 = 24.5$, p ~ .50
Order Zero Versus Order One $\chi 36^2 = 51.9$, p ~ .01
Order One Versus Order Two $\chi 9^2 = 357.$, p < .001

| | **Transition 4 (1965–67)** | | | |
	CS	**NT**	**NB**	**CB**
CS	.72 (10)	.14 (2)	.00 (0)	.14 (2)
NT	.06 (1)	.69 (11)	.19 (3)	.06 (1)
NB	.00 (0)	.09 (4)	.91 (43)	.00 (0)
CB	.00 (0)	.09 (3)	.09 (3)	.82 (27)

1958–56 Transitions Versus Fourth Power of Theory Matrix
(Expected Proportions from Fourth Power in Brackets)

	CS	**NT**	**NB**	**CB**
CS	.28 (.17)	.22 (.22)	.16 (.31)	.34 (.30)
NT	.05 (.16)	.47 (.26)	.18 (.32)	.30 (.26)
NB	.04 (.06)	.08 (.10)	.84 (.70)	.04 (.15)
CB	.00 (.06)	.08 (.09)	.57 (.57)	.35 (.28)

NOTE: Theory Matrix Versus New Transitions, $\chi_{12}^2 = 22.9$, $.02 < p < .05$. Fourth Power Hypothesis $\chi_{12}^2 = 15.5$, $.30 > p > .20$.

that (1) the stationarity notion makes good sense for this data; (2) the random walk notion can be safely rejected; and (3) we cannot reject the possibility that a chain with two-step memory would fit the data better than the fitted one-step memory chain does. At the moment we are not interested in pursuing the possibility of a two-step memory fit because of the small size of our data set.

Next, the new data from the most recent followup are used to test the Markov chain theory's predictive validity. Transition 4 (1965–67) should be compared entry by entry with the hypothesis provided by the stationary transition matrix. The new data break the theory, mainly because the diagonal domination of the latest transition matrix is much stronger than the theory allows. But, how sensible this is in terms of career psychology. In young adulthood the subjects tend to lock onto fixed aspirations far more than they did in adolescence. This greater stability has been shown elsewhere (Gribbons and Lohnes 1968) to reflect greater realism, greater satisfaction, and, one might say, the maturation of the development process. The rather stupid formal probability theory breaks down in a manner supportive of psychological theory.

A hard test for the Markov chain is to predict the long-step transitions from first observations in 8th grade to latest observations 10 years later. As shown by Kemeny and Snell (1960), the fourth power of the theory matrix renders such long-step predictions spanning 4 time intervals. At the bottom of table 4.2 these predictions are placed in brackets alongside the actual long-step proportions. The Markov theory stands up to this test rather well. It predicts that the NB group will be the only one in which a majority of 1958 starters will still be found in 1967. However, the actual long-step stabilities for all 4 groups are higher than predicted. Can career psychology explain this? Yes, if we note that the orientation dichotomy is sex linked and the colleging dichotomy is intelligence and social-class linked, and that these mediating variables are stubbornly enduring.

The acid test for a theory of human development is the accuracy of long-step predictions for individuals. Given the 1958 entry states for the 111 subjects, the Markov chain theory correctly predicts the 1967 states for 45%. These predictions are arrived at by assigning each

Table 4.3. Three Prediction Systems Compared

I. Markov Chain Predictions, Given 1958 Entry State for Each Subject and Fourth Power of Theory Matrix

		Predicted 1967 Groups			
		CS	NT	NB	CB
	CS	0	0	11	0
Actual	NT	0	0	20	0
1967	NB	0	0	49	0
Groups	CB	0	0	30	0
	45% Hits				

II. Psychometric Predictions, Given 1958 Sex, SES, IQ, RCP, and 1958 Prior Distribution for Career Goals Variable

		Predicted 1967 Groups			
		CS	NT	NB	CB
	CS	0	0	2	8
Actual	NT	4	0	8	7
1967	NB	2	0	35	12
Groups	CB	4	0	3	24
	54% Hits				

III. Psychometric: Markov Predictions, Given 1958, SES, IQ, RCP, and Priors from Rows of Theory Fourth Power Corresponding to 1958 Entry States of Subjects

		Predicted 1967 Groups			
		CS	NT	NB	CB
	CS	2	4	2	2
Actual	NT	1	10	5	3
1967	NB	1	3	39	6
Groups	CB	9	6	5	10
	56% Hits				

Table 4.4. Markov Chain Analysis of Educational Aspirations

Girls, N = 54

Markov	Educational Aspirations
Group 1	Graduate school; four-year college
Group 2	Junior college; nursing; vocational school; high school only; some high school

Initial Probabilities

Group 1: .41 Group 2: .59

Transition Matrix 1 (1958–61)
(frequencies in brackets)

	Group 1	1961	**Group 2**
Group 1 1958	.59 (13)		.41 (9)
Group 2	.16 (5)		.84 (27)

Transition Matrix 2 (1961–63)

	Group 1	1963	**Group 2**
Group 1 1961	.67 (12)		.33 (6)
Group 2	.08 (3)		.92 (33)

Transition Matrix 3 (1963–65)

	Group 1	1965	**Group 2**
Group 1 1963	.80 (12)		.20 (3)
Group 2	.13 (5)		.87 (34)

Stationary Transition Matrix*

	Group 1	**Group 2**
Group 1	.673	.327
Group 2	.121	.879

*Stationarity hypothesis $\chi_4^2 = 2.6$, p ~ .62; order zero versus order one $\chi_1^2 = 52.$, p < .001; order one versus order two $\chi_2^2 = .70$, p ~ .71.

Powers of Stationary Matrix for Girls' Educational Aspirations
Second Power (1958–63 Transitions)

1958	Group 1	.493	.508
	Group 2	.188	.812

Third Power (1958–65 Transitions)

1958	Group 1	.393	.607
	Group 2	.225	.775

Fourth Power (1958–67 Transitions)

1958	Group 1	.338	.662
	Group 2	.245	.755

Limiting Matrix (Equilibrium at 13th Power)

	Group 1	.270	.730
	Group 2	.270	.730

Test of Fit of Stationary Matrix Against 1967 Observations
Transition Matrix 4 (1965–67)†

	Group 1	1967	**Group 2**
Group 1	Observed .65 (11)		Observed .35 (6)
	Expected .673 (11.4)		Expected .327 (5.6)
	$\chi^2 = .01$		$\chi^2 = .03$

Table 4.4. Markov Chain Analysis of Educational Aspirations (Cont'd)

1965

	Observed .00 (0)	Observed 1.00 (37)
Group 2	Expected .121 (3.8)	Expected .897 (33.2)
	$\chi^2 = 3.80$	$\chi^2 = .43$

†Goodness of fit hypothesis $\chi_2^2 = 4.27, .25 > p > .10$.

Test of Fit of Fourth Power of Stationary Matrix
Against 1958 to 1967 Transitions‡

	Group 1	1967	**Group 2**
Group 1	Observed .455 (10)		Observed .545 (12)
	Expected .338 (7.4)		Expected .662 (14.6)
	$\chi^2 = .92$		$\chi^2 = .46$
1958			
Group 2	Observed .094 (3)		Observed .906 (29)
	Expected .245 (7.8)		Expected .755 (24.2)
	$\chi^2 = 2.96$		$\chi^2 = .95$

‡Goodness of fit hypothesis $\chi_2^2 = 5.29, p < .05$.

subject to that group for which the entry is the largest in the row of the fourth power of the theory matrix corresponding to his entry group. We have taken our best psychometric shot at this prediction problem by predicting the 1967 states for the subjects from their 1958 8th-grade score profiles on four variables (sex, socioeconomic status, intelligence, and vocational maturity), and taking into account the known 1958 sizes of the criterion groups as prior probabilities. This psychometric prediction system achieves 54% hits, which is a rather slight improvement over the 45% hits from the formal probability model. Note that the random walk, which would usually be used as a standard of comparison, would be expected to yield only 25% hits for this four-cell criterion (see table 4.3).

Finally, we propose to try to improve predictions by marrying the Markov basis to the psychometric basis. The psychometric: Markov prediction system employs the 1958 measurement profiles and the information contained in the fourth power of the Markov theory matrix, by using the row of the latter corresponding to each subject's 1958 entry state as the prior probabilities in his classification computation. For these data we achieve only a 56% hit rate, but we are convinced there will be data collections for which this combined prediction system will provide really improved hit rates. Then we will have an indication that a theory for the development process will have to take into account both a degree of inherent lawfulness in the criterion variable and a degree of covariance with a multivariate trait predictor.

Table 4.5. Markov Chain Analysis of Roe Level of Occupational Aspirations

Boys, N = 56

Markov	(Modified Roe Level of Occupational Aspirations
Group 1	1, doctors, high managerial; 2, professionals, managerial
Group 2	3, semiprofessionals, low managerial; 4, skilled workers; 5, semiskilled; 6, unskilled; 7, no aspiration

Initial Probabilities

Group 1:   .57   Group 2:   .43

Transition Matrix 1 (1958–61)

	Group 1	1961	**Group 2**
Group 1 1958	.75 (24)		.25 (8)
Group 2	.29 (7)		.71 (17)

Transition Matrix 2 (1961–63)

	Group 1	1963	**Group 2**
Group 1 1961	.71 (22)		.29 (9)
Group 2	.16 (4)		.84 (21)

Transition Matrix 3 (1963–65)

	Group 1	1965	**Group 2**
Group 1 1963	.88 (23)		.12 (3)
Group 2	.20 (6)		.80 (24)

Stationary Transition Matrix*

	Group 1	**Group 2**
Group 1	.775	.225
Group 2	.215	.785

*Stationarity hypothesis $\chi_4^2 = 4.0$, p ~ .41; order zero versus order one $\chi_1^2 = 53.$, p < .001; order one versus order two $\chi_2^2 = 4.9$, p < .09.

Powers of Stationary Matrix for Boys'
Roe Level of Occupational Aspirations

Second Power (1958–63 Transitions)

1958	Group 1	.649	.351
	Group 2	.335	.665

Third Power (1958–65 Transitions)

1958	Group 1	.578	.422
	Group 2	.403	.597

Fourth Power (1958–67 Transitions)

1958	Group 1	.539	.461
	Group 2	.441	.559

Limiting Matrix (Equilibrium at 14th Power)

Group 1	.489	.511
Group 2	.489	.511

Test of Fit of Stationary Matrix Against 1967 Observations†
Transition Matrix 4 (1965–67)

	Group 1	1967	**Group 2**
Group 1	Observed .82 (24)		Observed .18 (5)
	Expected .775 (21.6)		Expected .225 (6.4)
	$\chi^2 = .27$		$\chi^2 = .31$

Table 4.5. Markov Chain Analysis of Roe Level of Occupational Aspirations (Cont'd)

1965

	Observed .37 (10)	Observed .63 (17)
Group 2	Expected .215 (6.0)	Expected .785 (22.0)
	$\chi^2 = 2.67$	$\chi^2 = 1.14$

†Goodness of fit hypothesis $\chi_2^2 = 4.39$, $.25 > p > .10$.

Test of Fit of Fourth Power of Stationary Matrix
Against 1958 to 1967 Transitions‡

	Group 1	1967	**Group 2**
	Observed .719 (23)		Observed .281 (9)
Group 1	Expected .539 (17.3)		Expected .461 (14.7)
	$\chi^2 = 1.88$		$\chi^2 = 2.21$
1958			
	Observed .500 (12)		Observed .500 (12)
Group 2	Expected .441 (10.6)		Expected .559 (13.4)
	$\chi^2 = .18$		$\chi^2 = .15$

‡Goodness of fit hypothesis $\chi_2^2 = 4.42$, $.25 > p > .10$.

Fourth Transitions on Other Variables

In *Emerging Careers* we reported seemingly reasonable Markov chain fits for girls and boys separately on a dichotomous level of occupational aspiration variable, and for girls on a dichotomous educational aspiration variable. These fits were computed on the three transitions available at that time. Since then, the availability of observations for a fourth transition (1965 to 1967) has made it possible to test the predictive validities of the chains, with the following results.

Table 4.4 reviews the earlier results on girls' educational aspirations and adds the analyses of the new data. Note that in the 8th grade 42% of the girls planned to attend a baccalaureate college, but this percentage eroded steadily, until in 1967 the interviews showed only 20% aspiring to baccalaureate degrees. The theory matrix of stationary probabilities gives a girl who aspires to a college degree at any time 2 chances out of 3 of maintaining that aspiration over a 2-year transition period, while it gives a girl who starts a period with no college degree plans only slightly better than 1 chance out of 10 of acquiring such plans over the next 2 years. The limiting matrix predicts that finally only 27% of the girls will achieve baccalaureate degrees.

The new data on the 1965–67 transition are reasonably close to the predictions of the theory matrix. The greatest discrepancy is that in fact *no* young women who started this period without baccalaureate aspirations acquired such plans over the period. All the Group 2 members appear to be trapped there. The theory does *not* pass the hard test

Table 4.6. Markov Chain Analysis of Roe Level of Occupational Aspirations

Girls, N = 54

Markov	(Modified Roe Level of Occupational Aspirations
Group 1	1, doctors, high managerial; 2, professionals, managerial
Group 2	3, semiprofessionals, low managerial; 4, skilled workers; 5, semiskilled; 6, unskilled; 7, no aspiration

Initial Probabilities
Group 1:   .43   Group 2:   .57

Transition Matrix 1 (1958–61)

	Group 1	1961	Group 2
Group 1	.70 (16)		.30 (7)
1958			
Group 2	.23 (7)		.77 (24)

Transition Matrix 2 (1961–63)

	Group 1	1963	Group 2
Group 1	.70 (16)		.30 (7)
1961			
Group 2	.10 (3)		.90 (28)

Transition Matrix 3 (1963–65)

	Group 1	1965	Group 2
Group 1	.74 (14)		.26 (5)
1963			
Group 2	.03 (1)		.97 (34)

Stationary Transition Matrix*

	Group 1	Group 2
Group 1	.708	.292
Group 2	.113	.887

*Stationarity hypothesis $\chi_4^2 = 6.6$, p ~ .6; Order zero versus order one $\chi_1^2 = 60.$, p < .001; Order one versus order two $\chi_2^2 = 2.1$, p < .35.

Powers of Stationary Matrix for Girls'
Roe Level of Occupational Aspirations

Second Power (1958–63 Transitions)

		Group 1	Group 2
1958	Group 1	.534	.466
	Group 2	.180	.820

Third Power (1958–65 Transitions)

		Group 1	Group 2
1958	Group 1	.431	.569
	Group 2	.220	.780

Fourth Power (1958–67 Transitions)

		Group 1	Group 2
1958	Group 1	.369	.631
	Group 2	.244	.756

Limiting Matrix (Equilibrium at 14th Power)

	Group 1	Group 2
Group 1	.279	.721
Group 2	.279	.721

Test of Fit of Stationary Matrix Against 1967 Observations†
Transition Matrix 4 (1965–67)

	Group 1	Group 2
	Observed .47 (7)	Observed .53 (8)
Group 1	Expected .708 (10.6)	Expected .292 (4.4)
	$\chi^2 = 1.22$	$\chi^2 = 2.95$

Table 4.6. Markov Chain Analysis of Roe Level of Occupational Aspirations (Cont'd)

1965

	Observed .03 (1)	Observed .97 (38)
Group 2	Expected .133 (4.3)	Expected .887 (34.7)
	$\chi^2 = 2.53$	$\chi^2 = .31$

†Goodness of fit hypothesis $\chi_2{}^2 = 7.01$, $.025 > p > .05$.

Test of Fit of Fourth Power of Stationary Matrix
Against 1958 to 1967 Transitions‡

	Group 1	1967	**Group 2**
	Observed .174 (4)		Observed .826 (19)
Group 1	Expected .369 (8.5)		Expected .631 (14.5)
	$\chi^2 = 2.38$		$\chi^2 = 1.39$
1958			
	Observed .129 (4)		Observed .871 (27)
Group 2	Expected .244 (7.6)		Expected .756 (23.4)
	$\chi^2 = 1.70$		$\chi^2 = .55$

‡Goodness of fit hypothesis $\chi_2^{2} = 6.02$, $p \sim .05$.

of predicting the long-step transition distribution from 1958 to 1967. The problem is that both groups are more stable over the long step than the theory predicts them to be. This means that the 1958 educational aspirations of the girls are better indicators of what their 1967 educational aspirations will be than the chain theory based on intervening transitions leads us to expect. The distressing reality is that fully 90% of the girls who abjured college plans in the 8th-grade interviews still abjure college aspirations in 1967. This is really a self-imposed, self-fulfilling prophecy with a vengeance. Note that fewer than half the girls who expected in the 8th grade to earn college degrees still have this aspiration in 1967.

The picture on the boys' level of occupational aspiration patterns is more encouraging (table 4.5). Slightly more than half the boys started in 1958 with high aspirations, the limiting matrix predicts that almost half the men will have high aspirations when the process achieves equilibrium, and actually, in the 1967, data 63% of the young men profess aspirations to Group 1, or high level, vocations. The noteworthy feature of the theory matrix and of the first three data matrices to which it was fitted is their high degree of diagonal domination, so that in fact and theory there are about three chances out of four of remaining over a period in whatever group one starts that period in.

We see that the data for the 1965–67 transition match the theory matrix in distribution reasonably well. The differences are quite encouraging: more young men who had high occupational aspirations in 1965 have retained them in 1967 than predicted, and more who had low aspirations in 1965 have changed to high aspirations in 1967 than predicted. The theory also does reasonably well on the difficult task of predicting the distribution of long-step 1958–67 transitions. The discrepancy is encouraging because it lies mostly in a greater percentage of high-aspiring 8th-grade males who display that high aspiration again four years beyond high school than is predicted by the fourth power of the theory matrix.

The women do not fare as well as the men on occupational aspiration level patterns (table 4.6). Instead, their patterns on this variable are very much like their patterns on educational aspirations, with only 15% of the young women expressing Group 1 aspirations in 1967. The theory matrix does *not* predict the 1965–67 transitions reasonably well, because too few women maintained high aspirations and too many maintained low aspirations over this period. The long-step 1958–67 distribution is *not* reasonably well predicted, again largely because too few of the girls who expressed high vocational aspirations in the 8th grade have again expressed high vocational aspirations when interviewed four years beyond high school. The new data are discouraging for the Markov chain theory for these patterns but, more important, the trends in the patterns are discouraging for girls, who in early adolescence have high career aspirations.

Summary

We have turned to Markov chain analysis because we need methodology that treats patterns in time series on career adjustment variables as *patterns*. At least the chain model acknowledges the existence of a continuing process and attempts to describe its inherent lawfulness. The trouble is that the assumptions the chain model makes about the simple ways the history of the subject on the variable may affect his next observation value are unrealistic. Actually, we have in hand some Markov chain theory matrices that stand the test of new data better than one would expect. The problem is how to capitalize on what loose but reasonable fits of chains we can obtain. We have suggested using the best fitted chain as a null hypothesis, letting it account for what variability it can, and then asking what trait-statistical prediction can do to account for the remaining variability. Although we do not have a very persuasive example, we believe the new combined Markov: statistical prediction system we have described and demonstrated has great promise for longitudinal research on human development.

5
Six Case Studies

In our previous reports of the Career Development Study, people became statistics and their careers were factors for analysis. This "dehumanization" is necessary for formulating any scientific theory and we make no apologies for this approach. In this chapter, however, we return names to the numbers and replace types and traits with actual behaviors and attitudes from the subjects' own words, school record data, and the clinicians' impressions.

From the 110 subjects, we have chosen 3 men and 3 women, each of whose careers corresponds to one of the 4 Differential Career Processes. The data used in these histories were obtained from interviews with the subjects in the 8th, 10th, and 12th grades, and 2 and 4 years out of school. The 6-year followup was a mailed questionnaire and the 21-year followup was a combination of mailed questionnaires and telephone calls to our subjects.

We hope in these very brief case histories to demonstrate the value of our subjects' contributions, not only as statistical representatives, but also as real careers of real people. Perhaps this close look, albeit very brief, will encourage career theorists and guidance counselors to appreciate the value of their work and move forward to greater understanding of careers in progress.

The names of the men and women have been changed when necessary for concealment, as have their occupational aspirations and actual occupations, but they have been kept within the same Roe Occupational Levels and Groups as originally classified. In all cases, the data remain faithful to the "real life" activities of the individuals.

Degeneration: The Case of Carol

Carol's case represents degeneration, i.e., the progressive deterioration of aspirations and achievement, accompanied by frustration and loss of status.

The eldest of four children, Carol grew up in a middle-class community close to Boston. Her father, an accountant with a large manufacturing firm, had attended evening classes at a school of business, and her mother was a housewife who had graduated from high school.

In 8th grade Carol planned on being a teacher because she liked children and sometimes helped them with their lessons. Aware of the educational requirements for the profession, she planned to attend a four-year teachers college near her home and then probably go on for a Master's degree as her teacher of the previous year had done. She realistically appraised her abilities as above average and said she hadn't been getting high grades because she hadn't been trying. Carol took responsibility for her own decisions and said her parents agreed she should go to college if she kept her marks up.

By 10th grade Carol had abandoned her 8th-grade occupational choice of teacher and changed from the college curriculum to business. She said her algebra was all right but "Latin didn't come too easy." She had warning cards in that subject and made her decision to switch primarily on that basis. Her self-concept seemed to be deteriorating, and she said she was "average in everything . . . not doing poorly, but nothing spectacular either." She had decided to become a secretary, which would require only a high school education, but she knew secretarial school would help and she might go on for a couple of years. When asked why she made the choice of secretary she said that she'd like to work in an office but later added, "I like to be on the go a lot . . . don't like to be sitting down." However, she did relate her courses to her occupational choice and continued to take responsibility for her decisions.

Carol was still in the business curriculum in 12th grade and aspired to becoming a bookkeeper because it was so easy and she wouldn't have to type all day long. She was almost sure she would get a job directly after high school graduation because her father could get her a job with his company. Failing this, she would go on to business school, financed with money she had been saving and help from her parents who agreed to assist her if she decided to continue her education. Speaking rather wistfully about being a teacher, her first choice in 8th grade, she said, "Teaching is what I'd really like, but I can't do it." Although she said the most important factor in choosing a job was "if you enjoyed it," she had stated in an earlier response, "I don't like office work that much, but a girl who isn't smart can do it." Carol, who possessed an above average IQ, was losing her self-confidence and self-esteem.

Her favorite hobbies were making clothes, setting hair, and taking care of children. She said she would like most in life to get married and raise a family, that she had almost married the previous year but her parents had talked her out of it. It seemed that the past two years had been difficult for Carol in many ways and it reminded us that in the 10th grade she had said that it was important to be cheerful on the outside even when things are bothering you, not letting your feelings show. We wonder how different her life during those years could have been had she been able to show her inner feelings and discuss them with an interested, informed adult.

High school plus 2 years found a very dissatisfied young woman who was keeping accounts for a public utility. The job required no training: "They just showed me what to do the first day and I did it." She found the work boring and monotonous, and she just didn't like it. It would take four years before she could achieve any advancement and she hoped she wouldn't be there that long. If she wasn't married within two years, she would try some other occupation.

Still harboring thoughts of being a teacher, she said she enjoyed correcting tests for her boy friend who was a teacher and that if she could do it over she would go back to the college curriculum and become a teacher.

The happy ending to this story came in Carol's response to our high school plus six years questionnaire. She was indeed married (not to her teacher friend) and wrote us, "I lead the very normal housewife life. I enjoy being married and raising a family. I am very happy in my occupation." The 21-year follow-up found Carol still a happily married housewife and mother.

Emerging Maturity: The Case of Mike

Emerging maturity is the passage of a young person such as Mike through the stages and tasks of Super's developmental model.

Mike, the youngest of four boys, is the son of two semiskilled factory workers, neither of whom had achieved a high school education. He grew up in a workingman's neighborhood of multiple family dwellings, in an industrial town not far from Boston.

In the 8th grade and through high school, Mike's primary occupational aspiration was to become a business manager "like my brother." Although he had an average Otis IQ, he felt he was unable to do the work required by the college curriculum and chose business because it was easier. In spite of this, he aspired to a college education and failed to recognize that his high school choice was inappropriate for his educational aspirations. He felt that he, his parents, and his brother should be responsible for his choices; but he would change if his family didn't agree with his choice. Mike answered most questions about himself and his choices with, "I don't know," demonstrating very low vocational maturity.

When Mike was in the 10th grade he had begun synthesizing his needs, interests, capacities, values, and opportunities. Having changed to the college curriculum, he planned to attend a college near his home. He had shifted from business manager to biologist after having been employed part-time in a medical laboratory and enjoying his work.

At the 12th grade interview, Mike was enrolled at a private preparatory school and had reverted to his 8th grade aspiration of going into business management. He expressed some concern about his prospects of getting into college and worried about the possibility that he might be drafted. It must be remembered that this was the period of the Vietnam war and most of our young men shared this very real concern.

Our high school plus 2 years interview revealed a very difficult period in Mike's life. He had dropped out of school before graduation and was now attending night school to earn his high school diploma. He said, "Dropping out of school was the sorriest thing I ever did," and he blamed it on his buying and having to support a car. He was working as a janitor, an occupation he disliked very much but it was a means to an end. His 8th grade aspirations for a "happy family" had been realized and his plans, while vague, still included post-high school education.

Two years later Mike had achieved his high school diploma and was enrolled in a night program at a large university with full intentions of getting his B.S. He had become interested in an insurance course, which led to a job with an insurance company. He aspired to become an underwriter by the time he was 35. Formerly reticent to discuss his interests and values, Mike spoke at length about his new job, his family, and his optimistic plans for the future.

Mike's success as an insurance underwriter was confirmed by his response to the follow-up questionnaire 6 years after high school. He was working in the division of underwriters and had three people to supervise. He had transferred to a small community college and expected to receive his Associate in Science degree before the end of the year. He planned to continue his education by enrolling at a four-year state college full time to achieve his long-sought Bachelor of Science degree.

Our 21-year followup found a Mike who had completed his undergraduate work and achieved a B.S. in math. He was employed as a supervising underwriter and looked forward to a position in management. A Master's degree was also part of his future. The persistence he displayed in achieving his previous educational goals suggest that this too will be accomplished. Unfortunately, the marriage he spoke about with such pride and joy had dissolved as had the marriages of so many others of our young people.

On the basis of Mike's case history, we believe he was correctly classified as an emerging maturer, but we realize that his maturity emerged far later than we would have wished. Unfortunately, Mike went off the track before he completed high school; proper guidance probably could have helped him avoid the misery of "making up time."

Constant Maturity: The Case of Jim

The consistent, persistent, realistic pursuit of one's first stated goal presents constant maturity, the characteristic shown by Jim.

The older of two children in the family, Jim was brought up in an upper middle class home, in an affluent suburb north of Boston. Both of Jim's parents were college graduates—his father a prominent physician and his mother a housewife. When interviewed in 12th grade and 2 years out of high school, Jim expressed an awareness of the advantages of his home environment. "My attitude is that I'm a product of what I've been through. I have a brain and my parents have helped develop it properly. I've had everything shooting for me; never pressured about money, I don't know what it's like not to have it. I have a good family and can only imagine and sympathize with people who have family troubles."

Jim was first interviewed when he was 14 years old and in the 8th grade. Realizing that interests and abilities were important criteria for choosing a career, Jim spoke at length about them. His interests in the 8th grade centered around his vocational aspiration to become a scientist. When asked how his vocational choice satisfied his interests he answered, "I like to think out the impossible and figure out how it could be possible." Although he usually showed a realistic attitude toward his own strengths and weaknesses, he found fault with himself for being unable to "get to the point." This, in spite of the fact that he was extremely articulate and responded confidently and concisely to the interviewer's questions. It seemed, to the interviewer at that time, that he was searching for some weakness he could mention because all his other responses has been so self-assured and self-confident.

In the 8th, 10th, and 12th grade interviews, Jim consistently aspired to "getting the best education possible." Enrolled in the college preparatory curriculum in high school, Jim enjoyed science and math and saw no interest conflicting with, or a lack of fulfillment of, his career plans. He said he wanted to work near people, to keep busy, and to travel; he felt that as a scientist these requirements would be fulfilled. Jim realized the extensive education necessary for his career plans and persistently pursued further educational opportunities. Because of his family's advantageous socioeconomic status, Jim was able to pursue the best possible education without anxiety about financing it.

When Jim graduated from high school he stood in the upper 15% of his class. His general averages for his four years in high school were: English C (so probably he was basing his dissatisfaction with his ability to express himself on evidence of his grades), Math A, Science A, and Social Studies B. Jim showed on standard tests that both his quantitative and qualitative aptitudes were significantly higher than the mean. He scored in the mid 700s on both English and math College Boards.

Following high school graduation Jim was enrolled at an Ivy League college some 50 miles from his home. When interviewed during his sophomore year, Jim was already certain that his future would include graduate school, but he was undecided about choosing between research and consulting. He did say that he was more interested in business management than in laboratory work and he expressed self-confidence in his ability to communicate effectively and to help others to do so, indicating that he had overcome his previous dissatisfaction with his ability to express himself through language and was more realistic in his self-appraisal. Jim maintained a C average in his freshman year at college but predicted he would do honor work in the future. He accomplished this and was accepted at a prestigious graduate school of business. His decision to do his graduate work in business rather than science was, he said, because "applied research is too technical. I'd rather apply science to management and personnel work." Jim predicted that five years from his college graduation he would be involved in "organization studies in some type of consulting arrangement," and that at age 45 he would be "head of a company with about 100 consultants who were all experts in their fields." When asked for his positive and negative feelings about his prospects for work, he answered self-confidently, "I feel that communication is the business of understanding. Through management I can help people communicate more effectively and understand one another better. I am a little apprehensive of being under someone I consider incompetent."

Our last communication with Jim, the 21-year followup, revealed him to have been an early and accurate prophet of his future, for he was indeed president of his own firm of consultants in the field in which he had trained in graduate school and prepared for with 8 years' employment in a large corporation. Jim offers advice, much of which sounds to be a chronicle of his own career in progress, to young people of today: "At the bottom of things is hard work. It needs to be taught to kids that delayed gratification and hard work still pay off. The tendency is to think about being a whiz kid and it is not realistic. . . . this is a scientific and technological world and younger kids should not be so afraid of it. The back to nature stuff, while somewhat meaningful, is very narcissistic. We have to learn to live with and use technology, not run away from it for yogurt and sprouts." And especially interesting from a person who set his sights on a goal so early and persistently and successfully pursued it is this quote: "As a career strategy it is better to pick something, do it all the way and later, if it is not what you want, then change. Do not try to pick the best thing, it again is a myth because you change." While we did not attempt to assess job satisfaction, we note that Jim expects to be doing the same type of consulting five years from now, but with a larger group working for him. (100 by 45?) This would indicate satisfaction with his occupation, and we would certainly rate Jim's career as a professional success story, but we wonder at what price to himself because he adds, "Most high-achieving people are going to need analysis around mid-thirties. Many of their dreams become meshed in reality and no one told them this would happen. The first divorce and the first change of jobs is quite an experience."

Jim is an excellent example of constant maturity. He set realistic goals for himself early and consistently and persistently pursued them. Jim was a very fortunate young man in his family, his abilities, and in his superior education. It seems clear to us that our young people who evidenced constant maturity were least in need of formal guidance in high school, but they were often the very students who received the most attention.

Emerging Maturity: The Case of Susan

Susan exhibits emerging maturity, the passage though the stages and tasks of Super's developmental model.

When we first met Susan, the youngest of three daughters of a high school graduate blue-collar worker, she was a shy girl of 14 years. She demonstrated little self-awareness or self-confidence and had chosen the business curriculum because she felt she was "not smart enough for the college course," although she had an average IQ. Further, she seemed completely dominated by her parents, believing that she should go along with their wishes even if they conflicted with her own. She made her occupational choice of secretary because she believed "secretaries receive good salaries." By the time she was in the 10th grade she had changed both curriculum and occupational choices—her curriculum from business to college because she had decided she didn't want to sit and type all day and would need a college curriculum for her new occupational choice of nurse. Familiar with the nursing profession because her sister was a nurse and liked it, Susan said she would pursue that occupation even if her parents objected—a remarkable shift from her complete submission in 8th grade. By 12th grade Susan had downgraded to second place her choice of nursing in favor of medical technician, a consequence of her working part time in a hospital laboratory. She was decidedly more self-confident, less shy, and more articulate. This seemed to be a function not merely of chronological aging, but rather of an enhanced self-concept and growing independence. She said she had had a disagreement with her family and considered joining the Peace Corps. Susan graduated 72nd in a class of 200 students even though her grades showed a marked deterioration in 12th grade. Two years out of high school she was enrolled at a school for medical technicians, was sure she had made a correct career decision, and looked forward to going out to work. She was, however, hoping to continue her education with night courses toward a Bachelor of Science degree.

At high school plus 4 years, Susan was a working medical technician and enjoying her work, but still taking courses toward her B.S. Her strong sense of independence was demonstrated vividly in her approach to her work. She chose not to work for a single laboratory, dividing her time among three laboratories located in separate towns. Thus, she was able to make up her own schedule, sometimes working very long hours, but really enjoying her work along with relative freedom. From the 8th-grader who didn't like to read, she had developed into a woman who "read everything I can get my hands on." She was very interested in travel and was entertaining ideas of moving out of state. She had great confidence in herself and her work: "My work is really good." She regretted not studying in high school and said she had been a "borderline student" and she wouldn't be doing what she was doing if she hadn't been lucky. "When I was young I didn't realize about the future—or care. I needed some prodding." Susan's only criticism about her career was that she thought she was too young to be in the "rut" of working and that she should still be in school. However, she did seem to be a really happy young woman who was able to combine successfully both her work and her extra courses.

At high school plus 6 years Susan had achieved complete independence. She had moved to the Far West and enrolled in a state university. She changed her major three times, finally settling on public health because it enabled her to achieve her degree in the shortest period of time. She said her goal was not money but "an expansion of my own personal capacities." She continued to work in a laboratory because it gave her the funds to do the other things she wanted. She had become quite involved in politics, joining Students for a Democratic Society, working for civil rights, Biafra, and the Kennedy and McCarthy campaigns (the year was 1968 when there was much political unrest on campuses). She was happy with the direction her life was taking and planned to travel and not remain "stagnant" in any one place. Susan was most aware of the changes she had made and wrote, "I hope that I have not disrupted any pattern that you have made. My past remarks made to you in previous interviews have undoubtedly been influenced by previous personal ties. At the moment I am extremely independent in both thoughts and actions, along with great expectations for its expansion."

The 35-year-old Susan has continued to maintain her independence and sense of adventure. After receiving her B.S., she spent two years traveling around the world before settling in a foreign country where she has bought several acres of land. She continues her work as medical technician, still on her own terms, working for several different laboratories so she can control her own working time. She considered going to medical school but did not want to invest that much time away from her home. She says she would eventually like to combine farming with teaching music and dancing to young girls. Since she had always mentioned sports as her major interest and never mentioned dance or music before, this decision comes as a decided surprise for us. Susan's career seems to be a perfect testimonial to the fact that careers are in progress for a lifetime. Certainly few people are able to achieve the adventure and diversity that Susan has, but no careers are static. All change and develop.

Constant Immaturity: The Case of Carl

Carl represents constant immaturity, the persistent fixation on fantastic, unrealistic goals, with no advances in achieved level.

The second of four children, Carl is the son of a blue-collar worker who had not graduated from high school and a mother who was a high school graduate and worked as a checker in a grocery store. In the 8th grade his career aspirations were architecture, engineering, and mechanic. Rating himself in the third quarter of his class, Carl seemed to be a realistic and accurate judge of his own ability. He was unaware of many of the relevant factors in curriculum and occupational choices, but was planning to follow the college curriculum in high school. Although he was unsure of the educational requirements of the occupations he chose, he did plan a college education, which would have been necessary for his first two choices. He felt that his father, not he himself, was responsible for his career planning decisions.

Basing his decision on one low grade in the 9th grade and concluding that the college curriculum was "too hard," Carl changed to the business curriculum in the 10th grade. He had abandoned all his earlier career plans and aspired to become an airplane mechanic. Extremely impressionable, he had heard about a school for airplane mechanics in a classroom discussion and decided that "18 months of school, working outdoors, and repairing things," was exactly what he wanted to do. He seemed unaware that only a limited amount of the work would be out-of-doors, but he did recognize that there was "actually no connection between business curriculum and mechanics."

Coming under the influence of a teacher/coach in his junior year, Carl once again turned to the college curriculum. His occupational aspirations were also revised. He had abandoned his 8th grade plans to become an architect, saying he "didn't have the brains to be one," and now his 10th grade aspiration to be an airplane mechanic because he "didn't have the ability." It must be noted that he had done nothing by way of testing out his abilities in these areas in even elementary ways. In 12th grade he aspired to be a teacher and planned to attend prep school before going on to a four-year college.

On the whole, Carl's high school years were characterized by inconsistent educational and occupational goal seeking, by fluctuating indefinite plans for the future, and by dissatisfaction with his ability and with himself. Although his high school record showed that his performance was fair and he graduated in the middle third of his class, Carl usually judged himself to be a poor student. His advice to incoming high school freshmen implied what he probably considered to be his own most serious mistakes: "You should really stick to the books. The most important thing in high school is the studying. And don't let the little things get you down."

Two years after his high school graduation, Carl was a full-time preparatory school student and a part-time laborer. After high school graduation Carl had been employed at several temporary low-level jobs and was seldom satisfied with his work. He worked at "boring" jobs in order to earn money for school. Impatience and frustration at being unable to find a satisfactory job characterized his mood at this time. However, he also found school monotonous and boring and merely a means to an end, something to be tolerated until he could receive his degree. In retrospect, he wished he had taken greater advantage of school, blaming failure on his own immaturity and laziness.

In the interview session four years after high school, Carl revealed that he was married, that he had completed prep school, and that he had attended a two-year business school he had heard about from friends. He had used the school's catalogue as his major reference and had enrolled there because he "knew they accepted practically anyone." He added further that he had no evidence that he had the necessary ability for the school. He completed less than one year at this school because of financial problems and an increase in his family. Carl considered himself to be very fortunate in his wife and family. He still aspired to a four-year college education, which seemed very unrealistic and unlikely at that point. He was working as a laborer and was not happy with his career in progress. He said, "I'm 22 years old and no better off than someone just getting out of high school. It's my own fault." He wanted to return to school and his wife agreed that he should, but only nights, because he did have a family to support. He still thought he might be a teacher in five years. That seemed like a very unrealistic aspiration since he had taken no steps to implement this possibility and had no definite plans for his future education. Carl's future was unpredictable and his behavior consistently immature.

In a brief follow-up questionnaire six years after high school graduation, Carol wrote that he was employed as a real estate salesman and that his future occupational plan was to open a real estate office of his own. His educational plans for the future remained undecided.

Since Carl never completed any of his immediate or long-range plans during high school or in his post-high school years, it was difficult to predict his future development and success, but the prognosis was rather grim. It seemed he might never develop vocational maturity and might continue to allow events to control him by, as he said, "taking any job that comes along." However, the 21-year followup found a Carl who seemed to have achieved stability: he had been employed by one manufacturing company for several years and had climbed their job success ladder until he was district sales manager and hoped to achieve a position of regional sales manager in five years. He had taken various job-related courses and had given up his unrealistic educational plans. Perhaps his success in this occupation marks the end of the immaturity and vacillation that marked Carl's career during the first years of this study. Certainly many of the disappointments and frustrations he endured could have been prevented by instilling a more accurate and confident self-concept through counseling. With adequate guidance, frequent interviews, and encouragement, Carl might have achieved early vocational maturity and developed his career in a more satisfactory and rewarding way.

Constant Maturity: The Case of Maria

We include one case study which cannot be considered typical, but which is such an unusual example of the consistent, persistent, realistic pursuit of a goal we call constant maturity that we feel it will be useful and interesting to the reader. The subject's name has been changed as have some rather irrelevant details; however, because this profession demands such unique abilities and training, we have decided we must identify this 8th-grade occupational aspiration correctly as ballet dancer.

Maria, a very pretty and extremely serious 8th-grader, resided with her parents in a moderately affluent suburb west of Boston, where her father owned a small business and her mother was a housewife. Both parents had attended technical schools after high school graduation. At the time of our first interview, she had already determined to be a ballet dancer because she had been dancing for seven or eight years and she loved it. She knew she was good, that she was a "natural," and her teacher encouraged her to go on. She had chosen the college curriculum because she knew it would be an advantage even if she didn't go on to college, although she also realized that college would not be necessary for her profession. Her second choice was to be a writer because she liked that and had had some success in writing plays and stories. She was very independent in her decision making, saying that people should "decide on their own . . . not be forced, because they know what they can or can't do." She said her parents had enough faith in her to let her do what she wanted.

While Maria spent many hours a week taking lessons and helping other dance students, she also managed to do honor work and still take part in extracurricular activities. Except that in the 10th grade Maria had decided she would like two years of college, her choices and aspirations remained the same. She explained she had chosen the college curriculum to give her "freedom to branch into something else" if the dancing didn't work out. She had studied dancing during the summer in New York, and her teachers were urging her to continue because she had the energy and ability. If she had not had this encouragement from knowledgeable and admired people in this profession, she would have continued dancing as a hobby and gone on to something else, but it would have been difficult. Maria expressed her love for the profession passionately, "I love it—the joy of it, hours and hours a week. . . . Dancing is a form of expression like painting or writing. You can express any mood: sadness, happiness, silliness. I like the stage, behind the stage, and the people. It's nerve-wracking for a lot of girls, but I can't get out there enough. I love to perform." She was realistic and aware of the disadvantages—little chance for family life, hard work, constant studying, and low wages. To Maria, however, the advantages far outweighed the disadvantages because professional dancers "are married to their careers." She repeated the necessity for making one's own decisions and thought she would work out some compromise with her parents if they disagreed with her, but she would not give up her aspirations.

During her senior year in high school she was very active in the literary society and the student council and was made a member of the school's honor society. Her aspirations and determination persisted and she was successful in her career pursuits. She had already spent three summers studying in New York and had been invited to be an apprentice with a company there.

Our high school plus 2 years interview was conducted when Maria was with her parents for a very brief Christmas visit. She had moved to New York with the blessings and support of her family and pursued her studies, first on a partial, and then a full scholarship supplemented by earnings from various "jobs for the money." She said she was glad she had finished high school and noted that many of her friends had not and they regretted it. She would like to be taking college courses if she had the time and money, but she considered meeting students from all over the world an education in itself. Her career had advanced far more rapidly than she had hoped; she had been invited to join a professional company after one year of her apprenticeship and fully two years before she had expected it.

Maria's career continued to skyrocket and, by high school plus 6 years, she had received national acclaim as an extraordinary star with her picture appearing on the covers of several leading national magazines. She had traveled extensively, performed at the White House, and still considered performing a joy.

Because the professional life of a ballerina, like that of an athlete, is relatively short, we were especially curious to know how Maria's career, which had followed such a consistently straight track, was progressing. We were not surprised to learn that she was continuing to dance but that she had also obtained her license from the Imperial Society of Teachers of Dance and had studied Arts Management.

At the 21-year followup, Maria was assistant to the director of a professional ballet company, handling artistic and administrative business for the company. She continued to take a two-hour daily class for herself and occasionally taught ballet classes and rehearsals. Although she was working 10 to 12 hours a day, she said, "I love my work." She is happily married to a man in the arts and adds, "I've never been happier—with my life and my career." This is truly an extraordinary personal and professional success story of a career in progress.

6

Reliability and Correlates of the Revised Readiness for Career Planning Scale[1]

In the third phase of development of our measurement device for the assessment of the vocational maturity of 8th-grade boys and girls, a unidimensional personal interview consisting of 22 questions was administered to 121 8th-grade boys and girls by 6 student counselors. The interview schedule, titled Readiness for Career Planning (RCP), was a refinement of a 45-item interview developed in the first phase of the investigation. Alpha factor analysis revealed $\alpha = .81$ for the recommended simple scoring scheme, which the authors considered to be a reasonable, useful reliability. The correlations of total RCP scores with sex, intelligence, and socioeconomic status indicated that RCP was reasonably unconfounded with these standard research variables. The study verified that RCP scales a somewhat separate trait of adolescence with some promise of a vocational maturity measure that could be used by researchers and workers in the field of guidance.

We remind the reader that the Career Development Study (CDS) began in 1958 with the interviewing of a sample of 57 boys and 54 girls, 8th-graders in five eastern Massachusetts communities. A set of 8 scales, termed Readiness for Vocational Planning (RVP), was scored from the 45 interview items. The interview was readministered in the 10th grade and again scored for the 8 RVP scales. CDS maintained contact with all its subjects, except 2 who died, for 12 years, making their average age 25 at the last interview. A third phase of CDS was foreshadowed by the testing, in the second phase, of an alternative unidimensional scaling of vocational maturity in adolescence from a selection of 22 of the original 45 interview questions. This device was motivated partly by the need to recover degrees of freedom in the small sample situation, in order that vocational maturity might be teamed

1. Dr. Lu Pai is a co-author of this chapter.

with sex, intelligence, and socioeconomic status as joint predictors of career criteria. Repeated occurrence of approximately the same discriminant function based on the 8 RVP scales in the validity research also suggested a value for a unidimensional scaling solution and pointed to a certain subset of the RVP items as most useful. It also seemed desirable for CDS to provide the career guidance profession with a research and guidance tool based on a short interview and a simple scoring scheme. Thus, the Readiness for Career Planning (RCP) instrument was born. The third phase of CDS involved refinement of the instrument and manual, field testing in a variety of schools, and computation of reliability and correlations with other, standard indicators for a new panel of data. This chapter, reporting these updating activities, is intended to document the current status of RCP as a practical, proven procedure for measuring an aspect of vocational maturity in adolescence.

Revision of the RVP Scale

The CDS indicated that RVP was a promising instrument for assessing a student's ability to deal with decisions at the 8th grade, but administration and scoring proved too time consuming and cumbersome to be of practical value in today's schools. The product of statistical analyses and revisions of RVP questions and scoring procedures was the Readiness for Career Planning scale, which was considerably shorter (22 items vs. 45), and the scoring manual was simpler in both format and the criteria used for rating responses. RCP continued to emphasize questions that motivated pupils to reveal their thinking processes in making choices and to show their ability to analyze and synthesize accurate information about themselves and the educational and vocational worlds. Purely information-gathering questions were included to determine the pupil's awareness of facts outside himself that he must consider before he makes curriculum or occupational choices. Thus, the purpose for the questions in RCP was threefold: (1) To evaluate a pupil's ability to make accurate self-appraisal of her abilities, values, and interests; (2) To evaluate a pupil's ability to relate her self-appraisal to the educational and occupational worlds with realism and consistency; and (3) To evaluate a pupil's independence of others.

It is important to remember that the RCP was first a schedule for a counselor's interview with a junior high school student who was in the process of making a curriculum decision for her high school years. The youngster being interviewed was told that the purpose of the interview was to help the student and counselor know each other, and the student was asked to tell the counselor about her thoughts concerning future educational and occupational preferences. Therefore, even if RCP was not scored completely according to the manual, it was intended to be a useful, structured interview schedule for assessing the young person's readiness to make the important decisions he faces and to identify those areas in need of immediate attention.

RCP was secondly a rating scale for scoring the student on a dimension of vocational maturity. The special areas covered by the 22 questions in RCP were the following:

1. Reasons for choosing a curriculum or occupation (2 questions)
2. Awareness of strengths and weaknesses and their relation to the student's choices (8 questions)
3. Ability to cite relevant data concerning choices (5 questions)
4. Awareness of the relationship between curriculum choice and preferred occupation (1 question)
5. Choice of a curriculum leading to preferred occupation or allowing greatest freedom of choice in the future (4 questions)
6. Awareness of relationship between present interest and values to future occupational aspirations (2 questions)

A detailed scoring manual was provided to enable the counselor to become familiar with the rationale for RCP and the criteria used for rating the responses. The responses were rated on a 3-point scale based on the degree of vocational maturity they displayed. In general, a response was rated 0 if it was based on fantasy, authority considerations only, or was illogical or irrelevant. Scoring categories indicating maturity, 1 or 2 points, were based on relevance, accuracy, logic, and information. A counselor who had studied the manual and administered and scored RCP a few times would be able to score the items during the interview and have a total score before the interview was completed.

Sample

The 69 girls and 60 boys (complete data were available on 121 subjects) were junior high school students from 6 communities in 4 states. Their intelligence test scores ranged from 78 to 156 with a mean IQ of 110. Socioeconomic status, rated by Hamburger's (1958) revisions of Warner's scale, indicated that all 7 occupational classifications were included in the sample. The mean score of 3.46 indicated a tendency for the occupations to fall in the middle of the scale. All the interviews were conducted by 6 student counselors from Regis College.

Reliability of RCP

The questions addressed by the reliability inquiry were:

1. How close to univocal were the 22 items?
2. How reliable was a best, complex scaling of the major factor of the 22 items?
3. How reliable was the recommended simple scaling of RCP?

The question of univocality was vital because the RCP protocol was relatively expensive to produce, based as it was on an individually administered interview and judgmental scoring of the item responses, a process that might take 20 to 35 minutes to complete for each case. Although the interview yielded other information beyond the RCP score, it would be excessively wasteful to ignore the potential for scaling additional dimensions of behavior from the protocol, if such potential were indicated by factor analysis. Before this and the other two questions could be addressed, a choice of analytic tools was necessary. It seemed to us that Cronbach's alpha coefficient was the best index to the reliability of a behavior scale such as RCP. Alpha is an index to the correlation between the scale score in hand and an ideal score hypothetically derived from all the items of the domain of behavior (Cronbach 1951). With their invention of alpha factor analysis, Kaiser and Caffrey (1965) enabled us to extract successive uncorrelated factors from the intercorrelations of our items, such that alpha was maximized for each factor. The alpha factors seemed to us to have ideal psychometric properties. If we found high alpha coefficients for two or more factors, then we could not justify treating the interview as univocal. In fact, our alpha factor analysis revealed $\alpha = .70$ for the second factor and $\alpha = .61$ for the third. These were not useful reliabilities, and they indicated that only one scale could be scored usefully from this short interview protocol.

The analysis revealed $\alpha = .94$ for the first factor, showing that a highly reliable factor could be scaled from the 22 items. Table 6.1 reports the correlations of the items with the first alpha factor. Clearly

Table 6.1. Loadings of RCP Items on First Alpha Factor

1. Available high school curriculums	.46
2. Curriculum choice reasons	.37
3. Curriculum rejection reasons	.41
4. Advantages of college preparatory curriculum	.51
5. Advantages of other curriculums	.32
6. Necessary self-knowledge for curriculum chosen	.35
7. Personal abilities for curriculum chosen	.40
8. Personal deficiencies for curriculum chosen	.48
9. Required 9th-grade courses for curriculum chosen	.25
10. Factors predicting 9th-grade success	.41
11. Significance of algebra	.47
12. Occupational choice reasons	.45
13. Necessary self-knowledge for occupation chosen	.40
14. Education and training requirements of occupation	.31
15. Nature of work for occupation chosen	.52
16. Bearing of 9th-grade courses on occupation chosen	.40
17. Personal abilities for occupation chosen	.46
18. Personal deficiencies for occupation chosen	.33
19. Personal interests occupation would satisfy	.65
20. Personal values statement	.47
21. Personal values occupation chosen would satisfy	.49
22. Role of adults in personal planning	.40

some items related much more closely to the factor than did some others. Item 19, which asked the student what interests he or she had that the aspired-for occupation would satisfy, seemed to be the best indicator of the factor. Scoring this discovered factor would require the use of a complex of diverse weights for the 22 items, and we did not recommend scoring it. Also, since these weights were fitted by the differential calculus to the precise topology of the correlation surface for the 22 items as estimated from these 121 subjects, and the correlations would be somewhat different for any other set of subjects, this complex scoring scheme would not produce as high an alpha coefficient for any other sample. Under replication our α = .94 would necessarily "shrink."

It is against this expected shrinkage of alpha for the first factor that we evaluated the computed α = .81 for the recommended simple scoring scheme, using unit weights for all 22 items (i.e., simply summing the item scores to get a total RCP score), as acceptably good. Note that this coefficient of .81 was not subject to shrinkage. The simple formula did not capitalize on any chance events in the available panel of data, and would be as likely to increase as decrease in alpha analysis on any replication sample.

Table 6.2. Correlations of RCP with Standard Indicators

Variable	CDS Sample (N = 110)	New Sample (N = 121)
Sex	−.18	−.12
Intelligence	.31	.39
Socioeconomic Status	.14	.09
English Grades	n.a.	.33
Mathematics Grades	n.a.	.40

Correlates of RCP

If RCP was to be taken seriously as a scaling of a new factor of adolescent personality, it was important that it be reasonably unconfounded with the standard research variables of sex, intelligence, and socioeconomic status of family. This unconfoundedness prevailed for the original CDS sample and it reappeared for the new sample. Table 6.2 reports the correlates of RCP for both samples. The results were similar and reassuring. RCP might or might not be the important behavior trait we considered it to be, but at least it seemed to be a relatively separate aspect of personality.

While the predictive and construct validity claims for RCP continued to rest on the available reports of CDS, the new data analyses suggested that the protocol was best treated as univocal for scaling purposes, and that the recommended simple scoring scheme might provide reasonable, useful reliability. For the new data, the correlations with standard indicators were very similar to those obtained in CDS and they verified that RCP scales a somewhat separate behavior trait of adolescence, with some promise as a vocational maturity measure.

7

A 21-Year Followup

Early in 1980 a final data collection was completed. By this time the CDS subjects were 34 or 35 years old and were in the Stabilization substage of the Establishment stage of career development (see table 1.1). Useful contact was made with 91 of the 108 living subjects. This high response rate was gratifying because it testified to the value the subjects placed upon their participation in CDS, and of course it enabled Warren and Jean Gribbons to renew friendships which were now of 21 years' duration. It also allowed the testing of some of the career development propositions established earlier in the study and the drawing of some general conclusions.

In late 1979 when the decision to conduct a final data collection was made, Warren Gribbons enlisted the assistance of 13 student researchers at Regis College. Under the leadership of Jean Gribbons, this team of volunteers organized a highly successful search for the scattered CDS subjects. These young people gave so generously of their time and abilities in making this unfunded data collection possible that they deserve special honor and gratitude among the legion of Regis College students who have assisted the Career Development Study throughout its 24 years of existence. We salute our Regis College legion, front rank to rearmost, in words we borrow from the Seal of the State of Maryland: *Scuto bonae voluntatis tuae coronastinos* (Thou hast crowned us with the shield of thy good will).

Locating subjects with whom we had not updated addresses for over 10 years was difficult. Fortunately, we had asked all subjects at all interviews over the years to list at least two people who would know their addresses in the event that they and/or their parents moved between interviews. These listings helped tremendously. In some cases the 1980 interviewers were able to come up with new addresses provided by one of the names listed on the data card as early as 8th grade, i.e., 1958.

The first approach was to try to reach the subject by telephone at

113

the last known address. When this failed, as it did more often than not, the leads on the data cards were tried, sometimes necessitating 10 or 12 calls. If that approach failed, the research assistants went through several telephone directories and called people with the same or very similar names. On occasion there was resistance from family members or friends who were not sure CDS had permission to call the subjects, or who perhaps feared the call was from a collection agency. In a few such cases they agreed to forward letters to subjects for us. In all, 39 subjects were reached by telephone, and useful addresses for 18 others were obtained by calls to family or friends.

For the remaining cases, letters were mailed either to newly confirmed addresses or last-known addresses. In no single instance did the Post Office forward a letter for us, but two parents did so. When all these methods failed, other avenues were attempted. Letters to alumni associations of colleges attended by 6 subjects produced new addresses for 4 persons. One alumni director forwarded our letter without divulging the subject's address to us, and the subject responded. Several high school counselors were very cooperative, but only 1 solid lead materialized from this source. Two reunion chairpersons produced 4 solid leads. The first letter to subjects resulted in 25 responses, and the first followup letter yielded 7 additional responses. Overall, this search required hard, tedious, and sometimes frustrating work of the team members, but the reward of reaching 91 of the 108 living subjects more than made up for the difficulties.

The questionnaire requested minimal career information. We avoided personal questions, about such matters as marriage and divorce for example, and kept the questionnaire to a single page. We regret that we did not ask about occupation of spouse because it would have helped in assigning socioeconomic levels to subjects who were unemployed housewives. We focused on what the subjects were doing in 1980 and their educational and vocational experiences of the past ten years. We also asked for any thoughts about their careers that they would be willing to share with us, and were gratified to receive many long and detailed, even intimate, personal letters as well as seven offers to meet with us. One subject from California did drop in at Regis College when he was visiting his parents, and it was such a pleasant experience that we are scheming about how to have personal visits with all subjects in the future. Eight of the subjects requested information about CDS publications, and we sent them personal letters and a copy of a summary of the study. It is unfortunate that the requirement of protection of subject anonymity precludes our sharing excerpts from some of the letters we received. Some of our subjects have scaled extraordinary heights of achievement and experienced extraordinary career gratification, and some have told us harrowing tales of defeat and suffering. Behind the formalism of our analytic devices we are aware of real lives in progress in terms we cannot share with our readers.

Where Are They Now?

The original 1958 sample consisted of 111 8th graders randomly selected from 7 schools in 5 cities in the Metropolitan Boston area. The 1980 sample of 91 consisted of 47 women (87% of the original female sample) and 44 men (81% of the original male sample). In 1980 we found 67 subjects (74%) still living in Massachusetts, although 8 of these now resided some 100 or more miles from their original homes. Six subjects were now living in other New England states, 2 were living in foreign countries, and the remaining 16 were distributed throughout the U.S. and its territories. More women had left their home towns (14) than men (10), and 8 of these women had moved to distant states or territories: Texas, Hawaii, the Virgin Islands, California, Israel. We learned that 5 of the subjects we were unable to reach had moved to California or Florida. In general, however, the majority of the subjects had remained fairly close to their home towns.

Comparison of 1958 Aspirations with 1980 Occupations

Table 7.1 reveals that by 1980 very few of the subjects were in the occupations to which they had aspired as 8th-graders in 1958. Only six men and six women were in the same or closely related occupations. The importance of this finding is that it contributes to the invalidation of occupational titles as suitable rubrics for career guidance in secondary education. It makes very little sense to counsel youth about specific occupations that are likely to be of transitory interest to them. Talk about specific occupations should be for the purpose of illuminating principles that apply to discriminations among broad career fields and levels.

In 1958, 72% of the females aspired to 3 stereotypically female occupations: secretary (14), nurse (8), and teacher (12). Of the 14 secretary aspirants, only 3 are now in that occupation. Only 1 of the 8 nurse aspirants is a nurse, and none of the aspiring teachers is now in that occupation. At present 17 of the women are housewives, some of

Table 7.1. Comparison of Aspirations and Occupations

Males	1958 Aspiration	1980 Occupation
002	Aviation Engineer	Owner Remodelling Company
003	Electrical Engineer	Owner Business Consulting Firm
004	Engineer	Special Education Teacher
005	Doctor	Automobile Salesman
007	Lawyer	Partner in Law Firm
008	Navy	Data Processing Bank Officer
016	Accountant	Systems Analyst
017	Business	Auto Mechanic
019	Bricklayer	Production Supervisor
029	Engineer	Chief, Defense Intelligence Agency
031	Business	Minister
033	Scientist	Foreign Investments Analyst
040	Engineer	Sheet Metal Worker
041	Pilot	Elementary School Teacher
042	Scientist	Post Office Clerk
043	Engineer	Sales Manager, Trucking Company
050	Scientist	Electronics Technician
051	Ballplayer	Sheet Metal Mechanic
052	Doctor	Owner, One-man Business
053	Business	Design Draftsman
055	Journalist	Newspaper Delivery Manager
056	Owner, Gas Station	Liquidator of Banks
057	Doctor	Owner, Furniture Manufacture Co.
064	Musician	Unemployed Musician
065	Air Force Pilot	Policeman
066	Baseball Player	Unemployed Crane Operator
067	Draftsman	Owner, Night Club
069	Singer	Personnel and Sales Coordinator
076	Machinist	Insurance Salesman
077	Doctor	TWA Communications Worker
078	T.V. Repairman	Unemployed
079	Doctor	Accountant
080	Radio Repairman	Telephone Installer/Repairman
081	Auto Mechanic	Auto Mechanic
090	Mechanic	Truck Driver
092	Doctor	Embalmer/Funeral Director
093	Doctor	Marketing Manager
095	Janitor	Fireman
096	Machinist	Greenhouse Operator
099	Engineer	Electronics Technician
100	Mechanical Engineer	Electrical Engineer
102	Merchant	President, Commercial Stationery Co.
104	Engineer	Chemical Production Worker
106	Chemical Engineer	Payroll Supervisor

Females

009	Nurse	Housewife
011	Teacher	Rental Analyst, Oil Business
013	Nurse	Housewife
014	Teacher	Housewife/Part-time Bookkeeper
022	Secretary	Housewife
023	Rancher	Housewife/Part-time Grocery Bagger
024	Secretary	Secretary
025	Secretary	Legal Secretary/Office Manager
026	Secretary	Secretary
027	Secretary	Employee Benefits Consultant
034	Nurse	Nurse/Student
035	Model	Office Worker
036	Air Hostess	Housewife
037	Actress	Unemployed; International Marketing
038	Teacher	Assistant, Dental Business
039	Model	Elementary School Teacher
044	Secretary	Asst. V. President, Bank
045	Secretary	Dental Hygienist
047	Teacher	Waitress/Student
048	Teacher	Housewife
049	Housewife	Secretary/Word Processor
058	Secretary	Housewife/Student
059	Teacher	Housewife
060	Teacher	Histologist/Embalmer
061	Secretary	Unemployed
062	Singer	Singer/Band Owner
070	Dancer	Student Nurse
071	High School Teacher	Housewife
073	Secretary	Retail Systems Manager
074	Secretary	Housewife/Part-time Waitress
075	Teacher	Housewife
082	Teacher	Nurse
083	Marine	Chemical Process Specialist
084	Veterinarian	Receptionist, Private School
085	Secretary	Cashier
088	Teacher	Housewife
089	Actress	Mental Health Nurse
091	Nurse	Housewife
094	Secretary	Telephone Service Clerk
097	Nurse	Housewife
098	Teacher	Marine Biologist
101	Nurse	Asst. Manager, Dress Shop
103	Nurse	Licensed Practical Nurse
105	Nurse	Secretary
107	Secretary	Housewife
109	Dancer	Asst. Director, Ballet Company (was Prima Ballerina)
111	Model	Housewife

whom plan on re-entering the labor market, and some of whom had already achieved their occupational goals before becoming housewives and mothers. It was interesting that some women who worked outside the home listed that occupation, which was in some cases part-time or quite low-level work, and did not mention that they were housewives, although their parents had spoken of them as wives and mothers. These women may have been influenced by new pressures and expectations about what the role of women should be in our society.

Among the males in 8th grade, 59% verbalized a preference for 4 prestigious occupations: engineer (10), physician (7), business (6), and scientist (3). The great variance between those aspirations and the actual occupational outcomes for the males corroborates the theoretical proposition that in early adolescence these males were in a fantasy substage of the Growth stage of career development. Only 2 of the 10 engineer aspirants achieved that goal, and none of the 7 doctor aspirants became doctors.

Three men and 2 women were unemployed in 1980. All but 1 woman have faced major difficulties in their lives, as reported by their parents. One subject has been unemployed because of a work-related accident, 1 has never recovered from his service in Vietnam, 1 is a recovering drug addict, and the woman has been mentally ill for many years. In addition to these sad cases, we feel deeply the deaths of 3 of the men, 1 in the war and 2 in automobile accidents.

The categories of the Roe occupational group and level matrix can be used to analyze the data of table 7.1 in ways that are congruent with analyses reported in earlier chapters. The next two tables compare the 1958 aspirations with the 1980 occupations according to marginal distributions at the 2 times on Roe Level (table 7.2) and incidence of shifts in Roe Level (table 7.3). Table 7.2 indicates that the women experienced a sharp decrease in Level 2 (Professional and Managerial) classifications across the 21 years, and a slight increase (6 to 10) in Level 3 (Semiprofessional and Low Managerial) classifications. Roe made no provision for classifying the occupation of housewife, and we have arbitrarily assigned housewives to Level 4 (Skilled Support and Maintenance). Two of the women who were on child-bearing leave of absence in 1980 have been classified in the professions to which they intend to return. It is difficult to come to any conclusions about the women because many of the 17 who are presently housewives plan to re-enter the labor market, and some had already achieved their occupational goals before leaving the workplace to become housewives. It will be desirable to follow these women in the future in order to see how they fare on re-entring the workplace.

Table 7.2. Roe Level Distributions for 1958 and 1980

	Roe Level	Females 1958	Females 1980	Males 1958	Males 1980
1	High Professional and Managerial	0	0	7	4
2	Professional and Managerial	19	9	18	15
3	Semiprofessional and Low Managerial	6	10	11	14
4	Skilled Support and Maintenance	21	23	5	3
5	Semiskilled Support and Maintenance	0	2	3	5
6	Unskilled Support and Maintenance	0	1	0	0
7	Unemployed, No Aspiration	0	1	0	3
	Total Frequency	46	46	44	44

Among the men, we find no similar sharp shift in marginal distributions for Roe level. There is, however, a slight increase in Levels 1 and 2 from 8th-grade aspirations to actual 1980 outcomes.

Table 7.3 analyzes the stability of Roe Level classifications across the 21 years. It reveals that 12 men and 14 women remained at the same level, 19 men and 11 women achieved a higher level than they aspired to, and 13 men and 21 women failed to reach their level of aspiration. Once again, the men as a group fared considerably better than the women as a group. America cannot be said to have provided equality of opportunity for the sexes during the lifespan of these subjects. The best that can be said is that some of these women have fought through to impressive and satisfying careers.

We include Table 7.4, which compares the Roe Group classifications of 1958 occupational aspirations and 1980 occupations, with reluctance, because we know it does not give a clear picture of the development of group status for the women, due to the ambiguities regarding the status to be accorded housewives. Because Roe made no provision for the classification of housewives, we have arbitrarily as-

Table 7.3. Transitions in Roe Level from 1958 to 1980 by Frequency

	1958 Roe Level	Moved Up Fem	Moved Up Male	Same Level Fem	Same Level Male	Moved Down Fem	Moved Down Male
1	High Professional and Managerial	0	0	0	4	0	3
2	Professional and Managerial	0	3	3	7	16	8
3	Semiprofessional and Low Managerial	3	5	1	2	2	4
4	Skilled Support and Low Managerial	8	3	10	1	3	1
5	Semiskilled Support and Maintenance	0	1	0	2	0	0
6	Unskilled Support and Maintenance	0	0	0	0	0	0
7	Unemployed, No Aspiration	0	0	0	0	0	0
	Total Frequency	11	12	14	16	21	16

Table 7.4. Roe Group Distributions for 1958 and 1980

	Roe Group	Female 1958	Female 1980	Male 1958	Male 1980
0	Unemployed; No Aspiration; Housewife	1	19	0	3
1	Physical Labor	2	1	4	2
2	Social and Personal Service	0	0	0	2
3	Business	14	12	6	18
4	Industry	1	1	18	14
5	Math and Physical Sciences	0	0	5	1
6	Biological and Medical Sciences	9	9	7	1
7	Education and Humanities	12	2	2	3
8	Arts	7	2	2	0
9	Student	0	0	0	0
	Total Frequency	46	46	44	44

signed them to Group O (Unemployed or No Aspirations) according to a decision we made many years ago and now regret. We have maintained this usage to promote consistency with previously published CDS analyses, but we do not intend to suggest that housewives are unemployed or that they have no aspirations. What we have created is a catchall category of dubious meaningfulness. In a new life we would want to provide a separate category for housewives. Table 7.4 does show some interesting facts, however. All nine female aspirants to Group 6 (Biological and Medical Sciences) were in that group in 1980. None of the females aspired to Group 5 (Math and Physical Sciences), and none was in that group in 1980. One wonders how an earlier onset of the women's liberation movement and the drive for increased equality of opportunities for women would have affected choices in these two groups.

For men, the greatest shift was into Group 3 (Business), and the largest defections were from Groups 5 and 6 (Sciences). It seems likely that Sputnik and the onset of the space age in 1958 inspired unrealistic choices in the sciences for a number of the young males.

Socioeconomic Mobility

Socioeconomic status was rated according to the Hamburger Scale of Occupations. In 1958 the 8th-graders were classified according to their fathers' occupations. In 1980 the men were rated by their own occupations, the women who had full-time occupations by those, and the housewives by their husbands' occupations. Unfortunately the housewives were not asked for their husbands' occupations in the 1980 schedule, but several volunteered this information, and in the other

Table 7.5. Socioeconomic Status Transitions

SES in 1958	Class	1	2	3	4	5	6	7
		1980 SES Frequencies for Females (Males)						
1	1 (3)	1 (3)	2 (3)	1 (1)	0 (1)	1(1)	0 (0)	0 (0)
2	2	0 (1)	1 (0)	1 (1)	1 (0)	0 (1)	0 (0)	0 (0)
3	3	1 (1)	3 (0)	1 (0)	1 (1)	2 (0)	0 (1)	0 (0)
4	4	0 (0)	2 (3)	2 (5)	1 (3)	4 (1)	1 (0)	0 (0)
5	5	0 (0)	0 (4)	2 (4)	4 (1)	3 (0)	0 (0)	0 (0)
6	6	0 (0)	2 (1)	3 (0)	3 (0)	1 (3)	1 (0)	1 (3)
7	7	0 (0)	0 (0)	0 (0)	0 (1)	1 (0)	0 (0)	0 (0)
Total Frequency		2 (5)	10 (11)	10 (11)	10 (7)	12 (6)	2 (1)	1 (3)

cases the last recorded occupation of the husband was used. Undoubtedly this practice resulted in some errors of classification of socioeconomic status in 1980.

Table 7.5 reveals that 8 women and 6 men remained in the same socioeconomic class in 1980 that their families had occupied in 1958, while 24 women and 23 men moved one or more levels higher on the Hamburger scale. There were 15 women and 15 men lower in socioeconomic status in 1980 than the positions of their families in 1958. Thus, net gains outweigh net losses, and the transition patterns for the two sex groups are very similar.

Education

Table 7.6 reveals that only 20 of the 52 8th-graders who aspired to a college education actually achieved that goal. This may be the most striking distributive loss revealed in the entire CDS study, and we note it with sadness. No single male who had not aspired to a college education achieved that good, but three women who had not aspired to the baccalaureate degree actually achieved it. Most of our young people had to settle for 13 to 15 years of education (35), and too many ended their formal education with graduation from high school (33).

There was a dramatic difference in the number of males (32) and females (19) who aspired to college in 1958. Even more depressing is the comparison of the percentage of males who achieved that aspiration (54%) with the percentage of females who achieved it (16%). These discrepancies can be viewed as partly due to sex-role pressures on males and partly, perhaps, to some draft dodging via college exemptions by some males and the utilization of the G.I. Bill to help finance college by those who served.

Table 7.6. Years of Education Actually Achieved by 1958 Baccalaureate Aspirants

Actual Years of Education	Females	Males
17	2	8
16	1	9
14–15	7	6
13	6	3
HS only	3	6
Total Frequency	19	32

Table 7.7 shows that 24 of the 44 males (55%) were accurate in the predictions they gave in 1958 of the amount of education they would achieve, while only 13 of the 47 females (28%) were able to predict the amount of education they would achieve. The actual value of accuracy of prediction of his or her educational attainments by a person in early adolescence is open to question because of the danger of an unfortunate self-fulfilling prophecy, but concerning those subjects who aspired to a college education and did not achieve it, one has to wonder if some of them didn't deserve what they aspired to.

Predicted versus Actual Success Ratios

Life's die has been cast regarding career development for most of the CDS subjects. It is possible to give fairly conclusive level of attainment and coping ratings to the stabilized careers described in the 1980 data. These ratings make it possible to test the long-range predictions of Markov chain models fitted a decade earlier. They also provide a suitable final assessment of the panel of careers CDS has been studying for 21 years.

Turning back to table 4.6 reveals that the Limiting Matrix of the Markov chain for Roe Level of females made the long-range prediction that 28% of the stabilized careers of women would place their owners

Table 7.7. Educational Aspirations versus Attainments

1958 Aspiration	Educational Attainments for Females (Males) in Years							
	HS		13		14–15		16 or more	
HS Only	7	(5)	3	(0)	1	(0)	2	(0)
13 Years	7	(2)	1	(2)	1	(1)	0	(0)
14–15 Years	2	(1)	1	(0)	2	(0)	1	(0)
16 or More	3	(6)	6	(3)	7	(7)	3	(17)
Total Frequency	19	(14)	11	(5)	11	(8)	6	(17)

Table 7.8. Predicted versus Actual Roe Level Distribution for Females

| | Roe Levels | |
Source of Proportions	High (1, 2)	Lower (3–7)
Markov Chain Limiting Matrix	.279	.721
1980 Ratings from Data	.196	.804

finally in Roe Levels 1 and 2 (the highest levels), while 72% of the stabilized careers of women would place their owners in Roe Levels 3 through 7. This prediction of highest level career attainments for 28% of the women must be compared with an actual 1980 attainment of Roe Levels 1 and 2 by only 20% of the women. The Markov chain was somewhat optimistic but it did not miss the mark to a disastrous extent. Table 7.8 reports this comparison of chain prediction and actual attainment.

Turning back to Table 4.5 reminds us that the Limiting Matrix of the Markov chain for Roe Level of males rendered the long-range prediction that 49% of the CDS men would finally arrive in Roe Levels

Table 7.9. Predicted versus Actual Roe Level Distribution for Males

| | Roe Levels | |
Source of Proportions	High (1, 2)	Lower (3–7)
Markov Chain Limiting Matrix	.489	.511
1980 Ratings from Data	.432	.568

1 and 2. In 1965 when this chain model was estimated, this long-range prediction seemed like an impossible dream, but in fact 43% of the males attained Roe Levels 1 and 2 in the actual 1980 data. Again, the chain theory led to an overly optimistic prediction, but not by a disastrous margin. Table 7.9 reports this comparison of theory and validating data.

With some trepidation we have weighed each of the 94 cases for which we have 1980 information in the balance of our clinical judgment, and hazarded a simple "yes" or "no" rating of each case on the dimension of Coping Behaviors Adequacy. Despite the fact that we

Table 7.10. Predicted versus Actual Coping Ratings for 94 Subjects

| | Coping | |
Source of Proportions	Yes	No
Markov Chain Limiting Matrix	.500	.500
1980 Ratings from Data	.809	.191

chose to include the three deceased males with coping ratings of no, and despite an inclination to be tough (i.e., rate no) with all cases where we were in doubt, this operation resulted in 81% yes ratings and only 19% no ratings. That is, we judge on the 1980 data that four out of five of the CDS subjects have stabilized careers that incorporate successful coping adjustments. It seems to us that the career development process has led to successful midlife adjustments for four-fifths of the subjects who were contacted in 1980. (A caveat would be that we have been able to rate only 94 of the 110 CDS careers.)

Table 1.4 shows that the Markov chain fitted in 1967 had a Limiting Matrix that predicted a final coping distribution of 50% yes and 50% no. Our 1980 ratings dispute that chain-theoretical proposition, as shown by table 7.10. Even if our 1980 coping ratings err somewhat on the side of benevolence, and even if most of the unrated nonresponding subjects in fact deserve "no" ratings, so that a speculative 70 yes and 40 no (or 64% yes) distribution was thought likely for 1980, the outcome would be substantially more favorable than that predicted by the chain. It seems safe to say that life has been far more generous to our panel qua panel than the chain theory of table 1.4 predicted. Despite the gloom of our theorizing in 1967, in a distributive sense our subjects have done well. Their efforts on behalf of their own career development were better than our theorizing about them. We are pleased for them and congratulate them.

8
Implications for Education

People work to live. Regardless of what wonders of freedom from the necessity of work for the masses of humanity the future may hold, education still has to equip today's youth for psychological and sociological adjustments to living with the imperative of working. If education is to enable people to live in freedom rather than as slaves to necessity, it must show them how to transform a fate that is a future of work into a plan for a career. One primary measure of the success of education is the extent to which its clients go on to realize the satisfactions and render the contributions of productive careers. A life should be much more than just a career, and education should liberate intelligence generally, enabling adjustment to *all* the predicaments of the human condition, as well as cultivating understandings and personal initiatives leading to careers (Lohnes 1968), but for the moment we are constrained to focus on the latter mission. However, we acknowledge squarely, as should all guidance educators, that no career guidance program can possibly succeed in its special goals unless it is associated with a general educational program that liberates intelligence (Murphy 1961) and orients students to the great human predicaments (Tiedeman, 1978).

What should be the special education goals of a career guidance program, and what should be its methods? We have in hand lengthy reports on three major longitudinal studies of career development: the Career Pattern Study (CPS), brought up to age 25 by Super, Kowalski, and Gotkin, in *Floundering and Trial after High School* (1967); Project TALENT, as reported by Cooley and Lohnes in *Predicting Development of Young Adults* (1968); and the Career Development Study (CDS), reported on by Gribbons and Lohnes in *Emerging Careers* (1968) and further extended by this text. Although our thinking has been influenced by many other sources, we concentrate here particularly on the implications we see for education in the findings of these three studies.

125

What are the major findings of these longitudinal studies of career development? First, they have shown that career patterns can be conceptualized, operationally defined, measured, and predicted. Thus they have justified their eschewing vocational criteria for career criteria. Whereas the traditional vocational criterion was a single event observed at a single point in time, the career criterion is a transition in a variable observed twice at two different points in time, or a string of such transitions over several time periods. It has been shown that such transitions are in part predictable from probability laws fitted to the career process variables themselves, and in part predictable from antecedent trait profiles of subjects. From a prediction system that combines these two types of predictability, potentially useful projections of possible futures for guidance clients can be computed. Such computed projections have been called *prognostic probabilities* (Cooley and Lohnes 1968), and a computer measurement system (CMS) has been described that would produce them for guidance purposes (Cooley 1964).

Although a variety of career variables has been treated successfully in pattern analyses, the Career Development Tree from Project TALENT research appears to be the most useful mapping of career patterns over adolescence and into young adulthood, as we consider the needs of school guidance clients. A curriculum that would promote understanding of this mapping would produce a considerable sophistication in world view, which would then provide a frame of reference for explorations of personal multipotentiality in interaction with the CMS.

These researches, along with others, have shown that the predictors the CMS will have to incorporate as inputs to the computation of career predictions include:

Current Career Plans
Sex
Socioeconomic Status
Ability Factors
   Verbal Knowledge
   Mathematics
   English
   Visual Reasoning
Vocational Maturity Factors
Scholasticism
Interest Factors
   Science

Cultural
Business
Outdoors and Shop

CPS and CDS have concentrated on the assessment and validation of vocational maturity. The current summary of research from CPS states:

> Conceptually and empirically adequate measures of vocational maturity appear to be those which assess a boy's *knowledge of education and training requirements* for the occupations in which he is interested, together with certain other aspects of information, not so much because he will use those facts (or fictions), but because the possession of such information indicates an orientation to the world of work which will help him as the need for decisions, and for data on which to base them, arises. *Planning* is important for the same reasons, but less so. *Interest maturity,* as measured by Strong's Vocational Interest Blank, is also empirically sound as a measure of vocational maturity, [and] conceptually adequate because it measures similarity of interests to those of older [more mature] males. . . . (Super, Kowalski, and Gotkin 1967, pp. IX–17, 18)

We feel that CDS has shown how a structured junior high school guidance interview can yield a quantification of vocational maturity that can assist in the diagnosis of guidance learning needs and the making of decisions in the individualization of guidance services (see Appendix). Nevertheless, we agree that CDS and TALENT findings support this CPS generalization:

> (CPS research) brings out the fact that the standard measures which are most widely used in the schools and in educational and vocational guidance are the best predictors of vocational development in young adulthood. (Super, Kowalski, and Gotkin 1967, p. IX–18)

If the bright side of these researches is their pointing the way to better information systems for career guidance programs, the dark side is their showing that the majority of adolescents are poorly oriented with respect to career development tasks and that fully one-third to almost one-half of young adults at age 25 appear to be in career development trouble. For example, CPS concludes:

It is apparent that floundering is by no means an isolated phenomenon: approximately one-half of the job and training moves that a typical group of men make during the seven years after high school can be characterized as floundering. About one-third of young men can be classified as flounderers in this time period, and another fifteen percent flounder as often as they use more appropriate behavior. (Super, Kowalski, and Gotkin 1967, p. VI–37)

CDS results corroborate this directly, and TALENT results support it indirectly. Furthermore, summarizing data on occupation satisfaction at age 25, CPS finds among its subjects "a total of only about 55 percent who are more than lukewarm about their work" (Super, Kowalski, and Gotkin 1967, p. IX–6). A considerable threat to the objectivity of CDS data over the years has been posed by the frequency of overt requests for guidance from the subjects during the interviews. Statements of unsatisfied needs for guidance abound in the CDS protocols, as they do in TALENT's free-response sections of the followup questionnaires.

An axiom in our society is the vocational value of educational attainment. Education literally opens doors. These career researches combine to show in many ways that educational variables prefigure career variables. CPS now says flatly: "Educational level attained by age 25 was related to career success." (Super, Kowalski, and Gotkin 1967, p. VI–26) The question for educators is whether we really communicate this axiom early enough and convincingly enough to our young clients, especially to those who are not hearing it at home. We think it is in their failure to sponsor understanding of the career values of education that educators miss their main opportunity to promote the best career development possible in students.

Career guidance in our schools should begin in the elementary years with curriculum units designed to teach understanding and the value of careers and education as they intertwine in our civilization. In the junior high years, students should begin to interact with a computer measurement system that will help them to assess their personality and project their multipotentiality. Through curriculum units they should continue to broaden their understanding of career psychology and sociology. They should return to the computer interaction periodically to test the consequences of intervening events in their personal development and to make and revise decisions and plans. They should have access to a counselor who can help them with the emotional and subtle intellectual ramifications of self-exploration, especially when discontinuities occur in an otherwise orderly progress through developmental tasks.

Ways must be found to communicate the scientific knowledge we now have about career development to young people in our schools, in modes that encourage better relations of self to society, better self-direction and greater acceptance of responsibility for personal history. The knowledge is technical, involving probability laws and trait-statistical maps. It requires computer communication. We must have a computerized career information system as an integral part of a career guidance curriculum in our schools. Needless to say, we must also continue to expand and improve the enterprise of career development research, which provides the knowledge that is then translated into pedagogy by educators and into personal initiatives by students.

Finally, a word about the special career development problems of women in our society is in order, since half the subjects for CDS were women. (CPS and the TALENT studies cited researched male subjects only.) We have contrasted results for the two sexes consistently throughout our many tables, and the overall trend in these many contrasts is that our women, as a group, were able to aspire to less and to achieve less than our men. We know our women to be as valuable as our men, and we must insist that our society was less encouraging and supportive of optimal career development for our women than it was for our men. Sex-role stereotypes appear to have been the primary source of the special difficulties for our women. Our schools, and the career guidance programs within our schools, must lead in the struggle to destroy these stereotypes. Although the special challenge of finding ways to combine homemaking, childbearing, and child rearing with productive and rewarding careers in institutions and corporations outside the home must be met by women themselves, their education should provide them with the resources for doing so.

Appendix

New Readiness for Career Planning (RCP) Instrument and Manual

Because we feel that one major aim of counseling is to help the pupil integrate his/her accurate self-appraisal with information about the educational and occupational worlds in order to make wise choices and decisions, the greatest emphasis of RCP is placed on those questions that motivate the pupil to reveal thinking processes in making choices and to show ability to analyze and synthesize accurate information about self and the educational and vocational worlds. Purely information-gathering questions are also included to determine the pupil's awareness of facts outside himself that must be considered before making curriculum or occupational choices.

Thus, the purposes for the questions in RCP are, in general, threefold.

1. To evaluate a pupil's ability to make accurate self-appraisal in terms of abilities, values, and interests

2. To evaluate a pupil's ability to relate self-appraisal to the educational and occupational worlds with realism and consistency

3. To evaluate a pupil's independence of choice

Remember that the RCP is first a schedule for a counselor's interview with a junior high school student who is in the process of making a decision about a curriculum program for high school years. Secondly, RCP is a rating scale for scoring the student on a dimension of vocational maturity.

Listed below are the special areas covered by specific questions:

Questions 2, 12—Reasons for choosing a curriculum or an occupation

Questions 3, 6–8, 10, 13, 17, 18—Awareness of strengths and weaknesses and their relation to pupil's choices

Questions 9, 11, 14, 15, 21—Ability to cite relevant data concerning choices

Question 16—Awareness of the relationship between curriculum choice and preferred occupation
Questions 1, 4, 5, 11—Choice of a curriculum leading to preferred occupation or allowing greatest freedom of choice in the future
Questions 19, 20—Awareness of relationship between present interests and values to future occupational aspirations
Question 22—Importance of independence in decision-making process

Administering the RCP Instrument

Based on experiences with the original RVP 8th-grade interviews and comments from interviewers involved in the 1976 study, the following suggestions for using RCP should be adhered to as closely as possible.

1. Normally the interview should occur in the first part of the 8th grade or, if the timing of program differentiation in the school system involved so indicates, early in the 7th or 9th grade. Then, the questions should be phrased in terms of the 8th- or 10th-grade programs and courses. Such terms as "program" and "course" employed in the schedule should be changed to such terms as "curriculum" and "subject" to comply with local usage.

2. When the student arrives for the interview, he/she should be told that he is participating in a career development study and answers to the questions will help young people in the future make the best possible educational and vocational decisions for them. If RCP is being used in a research project, the subject must be assured that all responses are held in complete confidence and names are never used in connection with any reports on the study. The student should be told that the purpose of the interview is to help the student and the counselor know each other and to have the student tell the counselor about some of his/her thoughts concerning future educational and occupational preferences. This last point is extremely important because students are often told they are going for a test, or they infer this from comments of other students who have been interviewed. The question of a test may also arise as the counselor checks the score for each item. We have tried to de-emphasize the importance of the score by leaving three lines to the right of each question for quick marks as the interview proceeds. The three checks represent, from left to right, scores of 0, 1, and 2. The counselor need only add the middle scores of 1 point each and the right scores of 2 points each to obtain a total score.

3. As in any interview situation, good rapport is essential. Answer all questions the student may have about the interview schedule without giving him any leads or answers to the questions. Do not hesitate to suggest that many students have difficulties in answering some of these questions. It is all right to say, "Yes, that was a tough question," when the student seems upset at not being able to respond. This is particularly relevant with the value questions. The interviewer must be especially cautious at this point not to provide students with cues that will vitiate the scoring of the item. If a student's response does not provide enough information to score any item or he/she appears reluctant or shy about answering, you might try prompting with, "Tell me more. . . . Would you add to that answer. . . . What do you mean by?" You must remember, however, that we are measuring vocational maturity, and not all students will have responses to all questions.

The wording of some questions may seem rather harsh, but these questions can be softened by tone of voice. Also, please note that Yes/No questions have been avoided because the richest information about the thinking process comes through responses to open-ended questions.

Since this is not a vocabulary test, words not understood should be defined, but the counselor must be careful not to define, re-state, or re-word in such a way that the results of the interview will fail to measure accurately the student's vocational maturity.

Most of the difficulties discussed in this session will be overcome if the counselor studies the RCP questions and is familiar with the scoring criteria.

4. Interview time ranges from 12 to 40 minutes. Until the counselor or research person is familiar with the scoring criteria, an attempt should be made to be as detailed as possible in writing the student's responses. This will insure a complete protocol that can be scored after the interview has been completed. We expect a counselor who has administered RCP a few times to be able to rate each of the responses for degree of maturity as soon as the student's completes his/her response and to total the item scores immediately following the session.

5. The counselor must exercise particular skill with a student who does not express a program choice or occupational aspiration during the classification portion of the interview. Some students will have good reasons for not answering one or both of these questions, yet they will be penalized in the RCP scoring if they do not have at least tentative plans or aspirations. Therefore, such a student should be encouraged, but not forced, to express tentative preferences.

A student who is unable to respond to questions regarding curriculum preferences or occupational aspirations has not, of course, involved herself in the decision-making process that will be so important to her future. The counselor might want to continue with RCP; pointing out to the student that many youngsters are able to respond may provide enough motivation for the student to become involved in planning for her future.

6. Because students sometimes feel the questions are repetitious, especially about abilities in relation to curriculum and occupational choices, it is advisable to stress the words "curriculum" and "occupation." If necessary, say, "Some of the questions may sound the same, but please do respond as fully as possible to every question."

Criteria for Rating RCP Responses

For items 2–6, and 11–13; the response is rated for the degree of vocational maturity it displays as follows:

Rating	Judged Nature of Responses
0	Immature—based on fantasy or authority considerations only; illogical; irrelevant
1	Mature—based on one or more relevant and logical considerations drawn from *only one* of the three classes of factors listed below
2	Superior—based on two or more relevant and logical considerations drawn from *at least two* of the three classes of factors listed below

The three classes of factors for consideration in choosing and planning are:

Class 1   Personal abilities

Class 2   Personal values, interests, needs

Class 3   Social values and institutional procedures; social pressure

For Items 7, 8, 10, and 14–21; the response is rated according to the number of mature considerations it contains, as follows:

Rating	Judged Nature of Response
0	Immature—no relevant and logical consideration
1	Mature—*one* relevant and logical consideration
2	Superior—*two or more* relevant and logical considerations

For Items 1 and 9, the response is rated according to the correctness and completeness of information it contains, as follows:

Rating	Judged Nature of Response
0	Immature—no correct information, or only one piece of correct information
1	Mature—*two or more* pieces of correct information, but less than the total list or a full representation
2	Superior—a full list of correct information, or a full representation

Question 22, on autonomy of planning, is rated as follows:

Rating	Judged Nature of Response
0	Childish dependence, or childish rebellion at adult authority
1	Statement of appreciation of need for adult counsel, or statement of need for emerging self-direction and autonomy
2	Statement of *both* need for adult counsel *and* need for emerging self-direction and autonomy

Interpretation of RCP Scores

We feel that the interview is relatively easy to score and that it can provide the counselor with a good picture of the student's ability to deal with educational and vocational decisions.

Table 1 provides a guide for interpreting scores. The maximum score that can be obtained on RCP is 44 points. The mean score for the 121 students is 21. Table 1 ranks scores in both percentiles and quartiles, but we feel quartile scores would be more valuable to use, until more normative data are available. Students with scores of 25 and above are in the fourth quartile, and those with scores of 15 and below are in the first quartile.

Table 1. Readiness for Career Planning
(Conversion of Raw Scores to Percentile-Quartile Bank)

Raw Score	Percentile Grade 8	Quartile
37	99	4
33	99	
32	98	
31	97	
30	96	
29	94	
28	91	
27	83	
25	76	4
24	68	(Median) 3
21	49	2
20	44	
19	38	
18	33	
17	25	
16	22	2
15	18	1
14	13	
13	9	
11	8	
10	5	
9	3	
6	2	
5	1	1

Readiness for Career Planning Interview Schedule
Warren D. Gribbons and   Paul R. Lohnes
Regis College   SUNY at Buffalo

Interviewer:_____

Student's Name:_____   School:_____
Sex: M F Birthdate:_____   Date:_____
  I. Do you plan to finish high school?   Yes   No

II. Do you have any plans to go on to school after   Yes   No
you graduate from high school?

III. What school are you planning on? (Or kind of school, if response does not indicate.)

IV. How many years do you plan to go to school after high school?

V. At the present time what is your first preference for an occupation after you have completed your education?
Do you have a second preference in case you change your mind about being a _____? Second choice: _____

General conclusions about rapport with student, reactions to interview, etc.:

1. At the 9th (or appropriate) grade, students have to make a choice among several different curricula or programs for their high school years. Could you tell me what these programs are called?   _____ _____ _____
(If no response to Question 1, ask the following questions.)
    a) What are the names of the courses a student can take in high school?
    b) Does your school have special names for groups of these courses?
    c) What courses would you have to take if you wanted to go to college after high school?
    d) What courses would you have to take if you wanted to go into the business world?
    e) What courses would you have to take if you wanted to go into one of the skilled trades?
    f) Which of these courses do you think you'll take?

2. Why have you decided to take the _____ curriculum?   _____ _____ _____

3. Would you tell me why you have decided not to take the other programs available to you?   _____ _____ _____

4. Can you think of any advantages of taking the college preparatory program?   _____ _____ _____

5. Can you tell me any advantages of taking the other programs?   _____ _____ _____

6. What should you know about yourself before choosing your high school program?   _____ _____ _____

7. What abilities do you have that will help you to be successful in your high school program? (Prompt: Abilities are your strengths, things you do well.)   _____ _____ _____

8. What abilities do you wish you had that might make the _____ curriculum easier for you? (Prompt: What things do you have trouble with?)   _____ _____ _____

9. What courses must everyone who chooses the _____ program take in the 9th grade? (May have been answered, but score here.)   _____ _____ _____

10. How can you predict your chances of success in your 9th-grade courses? (Prompt: How can you tell ahead of time how well you'll do in some new courses in high school?)   _____ _____ _____

11. What differences does it make if you take algebra (geometry, if offered in 9th grade) or another math course in 9th grade?   _____ _____ _____

12. You told me earlier in this interview that you thought you would like to become a _____.
Would you tell me why you'd like to be a _____?   _____ _____ _____

13. Would you tell me what you should know about yourself before choosing an occupation?   _____ _____ _____

14. In the next few questions, I'm going to ask about your chosen occupation. Please assume I don't know anything about this occupation and answer with as much detail as possible.
What education and/or training are required to be a _____?   _____ _____ _____

15. What does a _____ do at work?   _____ _____ _____

16. What connection or relationship do you

see between the courses you'll be taking
in 9th grade and your work as a_____? ___ ___ ___

17. What abilities or skills do you have that
will help you to be successful in the work
you are planning? (Prompt: That is, anything you are good at that will help you be
a good _____.) ___ ___ ___

18. What abilities do you wish you had that
you feel would be important to a _____? ___ ___ ___

19. What particular interests do you have that
being a _____ would satisfy?
(Prompt: What interests do you have that
you could continue in your work?) ___ ___ ___

20. Things that are important to us are called
values. What are some of your values?
(Prompt: For example, an actor might
value fame, a politician might value
power.) ___ ___ ___

21. What values of yours would working as a
_____ satisfy? ___ ___ ___

22. What part should adults—your parents
and teachers—play in your planning for
the future? ___ ___ ___

RCP Total ___ ___ ___

References

Anderson, T. W., and Goodman, L. A. 1957 Statistical inference about Markov chains. *Annals of Mathematical Statistics* 28: 89–110.

Ansell, E. M., and Hansen, J. C. 1977. Patterns in vocational development of urban youth. In *Vocational Guidance and Career Development*, H. J. Peters and J. C. Hansen. ed. New York: Macmillan.

Cooley, W. W. 1964. A computer-measurement system for guidance. *Harvard Educational Review*, 34: 559–72.

Cooley, W. W., and Lohnes, P. R. 1962. *Multivariate procedures for the behavioral sciences.* New York: Wiley.

Cooley, W. W., and Lohnes, P. R. 1968. *Predicting development of young adults*. Palo Alto: American Institutes for Research.

Crites, J. O. 1965. Measurement of vocational maturity in adolescence attitude test of the vocational development inventory. *Psychological Monographs* 79 2: No. 595.

Crites, J. O. 1968. *Vocational psychology*. New York: McGraw-Hill.

Crites, J. O. 1974. The career maturity inventory. In *Measuring Vocational Maturity for Counseling and Evaluation*, D. E. Super, ed. Washington, DC: National Vocational and Guidance Association.

Cronbach, L. J. 1951. Coefficient alpha and the internal structure of tests. *Psychometrika* 16: 297–334.

Forest, D. J., and Thompson, A. S. 1974. The career development inventory. In *Measuring vocational maturity for counseling and evaluation*, D. E. Super Ed. Washington, DC: National Vocational Guidance Association.

Ginzberg, E. et al. 1951. *Occupational choice*. New York: Columbia University Press.

Gribbons, W. D. 1960. Evaluation of an eighth grade group guidance program. *Personnel Guidance Journal* 38: 740–45.

Gribbons, W. D. 1964. Changes in readiness for vocational planning from the eighth to the tenth grade. *Personnel Guidance Journal* 41: 908–913.

Gribbons, W. D., and Lohnes, P. R. 1964. Relationships among measures of readiness for vocational planning. *Journal of Counseling Psychology* 11: 13–19.

Gribbons, W. D., and Lohnes, P. R. 1964. Validation of vocational planning interview scales. *Journal of Counseling Psychology* 11: 20–26.

Gribbons, W. D., and Lohnes, P. R. 1965. Predicting five years' development in adolescents from readiness for vocational planning scales. *Journal of Educational Psychology* 56: 244–53.

Gribbons, W. D., and Lohnes, P. R. 1965. Shifts in adolescents' vocational values. *Personnel Guidance Journal* 44: 248–52.

Gribbons, W. D., and Lohnes, P. R. 1966. Occupational preferences and measured intelligence. *Vocational Guidance Quarterly* 14: 211–14.

Gribbons, W. D., and Lohnes, P. R. 1966. A five year study of students' educational aspirations. *Vocational Guidance Quarterly* 15: 66–70.

Gribbons, W. D., and Lohnes, P. R. 1966. *Career development.* Cooperative Research Project No. 5–0088. Weston, MA: Regis College.

Gribbons, W. D., and Lohnes, P. R. 1968. *Emerging careers.* New York: Teachers College Press.

Gribbons, W. D., and Lohnes, P. R. 1969. *Career development from age 13 to age 25.* Cooperative Research Project No. 6–2151. Weston, MA: Regis College (ERIC Document Reproduction Service, No. ED 040477).

Hamburger, M. 1958. Realism and consistency in early adolescent aspirations and expectations. Doctoral dissertation, Columbia University.

Hansen, J. C., and Ansell, E. R. 1973. Assessment of vocational maturity. *Journal of Vocational Behavior* 3: 89–94.

Holland, J. L., and Whitney, D. R. 1969. Career development. *Review of Educational Research* 39: 227–37.

Jordaan, J. P., and Heyde, M. B. 1979. *Vocational maturity during the high school years.* New York: Teachers College Press.

Kaiser, H. F., and Caffrey, J. 1965. Alpha factor analysis. *Psychometrika* 30: 1–14.

Katz, M. R. 1958. *You: Today and tomorrow.* Princeton: Educational Testing Service.

Katz, M. R. 1963. *Decisions and values.* New York: College Entrance Examination Board.

Kemeny, J. G., and Snell, J. L. 1960. *Finite Markov chains.* New York: Van Nostrand.

Lohnes, P. R. 1965. Markov models for human development research. *Journal of Counseling Psychology* 12: 322–27.

Lohnes, P. R. 1966. *Measuring adolescent personality.* Pittsburgh: American Institutes for Research.

Lohnes, P. R. 1968. Reformation through measurement in secondary education. *Proceedings of the 1967 Invitational Conference on Testing Problems.* Princeton: Educational Testing Service, pp. 102–121.

Murphy, G. 1961. *Freeing intelligence through teaching.* New York: Harper.

Osipow, S. H. 1968. *Theories of career development.* New York: Appleton-Century-Crofts.

Pincus, M. 1968. Toward operationalization of sense of agency. Mimeographed. Cambridge: ISVD, Harvard Graduate School of Education.

Roe, A., and Siegelman, M. 1964. *The origin of interests.* Washington, DC: American Personnel and Guidance Association.

Rulon, P. J., et al. 1967. *Multivariate statistics for personnel classification*. New York: Wiley.

Super, D. E. 1953. A theory of vocational development. *American Psychologist* 8: 185–90.

Super, D. E. 1963. The definition and measurement of early career behavior: A first formulation. *Personnel and Guidance Journal* 42: 775–80.

Super, d. E., et al. 1957. *Vocational development: A framework for research*. New York: Teachers College Press.

Super, D. E., and Overstreet, P. L. 1960. *The vocational maturity of ninth-grade boys*. New York: Teachers College Press.

Super, D. E., et al. 1963. *Career development: Self-concept theory*. New York: College Entrance Examination Board.

Super, D. E., Kowalski, R. S., and Gotkin, E. H. 1967. *Floundering and trial after high school*. New York: Teachers College Press, Columbia University.

Super, D. E., ed. 1974. *Measuring vocational maturity for counseling and evaluation*. Washington, DC: National Vocational Guidance Association.

Super, D. E., and Hall, D. T. 1978. Career development: Exploration and planning. In M. R. Rosenzweig and L. W. Porter, ed. *Annual Review of Psychology,* 29: 333–72.

Tiedeman, D. V., and Sternberg, J. J. 1952. Information appropriate for curriculum guidance. *Harvard Educational Review* 22: 257–74.

Tiedeman, D. V., and O'Hara, R. P. 1963. *Career development: Choice and adjustment*. New York: College Entrance Examination Board.

Westbrook, B. W., and Mastie, M. M. 1974. The cognitive maturity test. In *Measuring vocational maturity for counseling and Evaluation,* D. E. Super, ed. Washington, DC: National Vocational Guidance Association.

Index